In a Human Voice

In memory of my mother, Mabel Caminez Friedman, who taught me to listen for the voice under the conversation.

Carol Gilligan

In a Human Voice

polity

First published in 2023 by Polity Press

Polity Press
65 Bridge Street
Cambridge CB2 1UR, UK

Polity Press
111 River Street
Hoboken, NJ 07030, USA

ISBN-13: 978-1-5095-5678-6
ISBN-13: 978-1-5095-5679-3(pb)

A catalogue record for this book is available from the British Library.

Library of Congress Control Number: 2022951310

Typeset in 11 on 14pt Sabon
by Cheshire Typesetting Ltd, Cuddington, Cheshire
Printed and bound in Great Britain by CPI Group (UK) Ltd, Croydon

The publisher has used its best endeavours to ensure that the URLs for external websites referred to in this book are correct and active at the time of going to press. However, the publisher has no responsibility for the websites and can make no guarantee that a site will remain live or that the content is or will remain appropriate.

Every effort has been made to trace all copyright holders, but if any have been overlooked the publisher will be pleased to include any necessary credits in any subsequent reprint or edition.

For further information on Polity, visit our website:
politybooks.com

Contents

Preface

The immediate occasion for this book is the 40th anniversary of *In a Different Voice* and the 45th of the initial essay "In a Different Voice," published by the *Harvard Educational Review* in 1977. The deeper provocation was the coalescing of the insight that led me to change my title.

I had been coming to this insight over a number of years, prompted by new research and changes in the social/political climate. What surprised me was how long it had taken me to see what, in retrospect, seems obvious: the voice of care ethics is a human voice and the gendering of a human voice as "feminine" is a problem. In coming to this clarity, I often had the sense of trying to make my way through a thicket. Hearing the "different voice" as a human voice meant clearing away a series of impediments that stood in the way of seeing that the gender binary – the construction of human capabilities as either "masculine" or "feminine" – is not only a distortion of reality, but a cornerstone of patriarchy. This book takes its impetus from all that follows from, and is clarified by, this realization.

In laying out the path I followed in coming to this more intricate joining of the psychological with the political, I have brought new writing together with recent works that became stepping stones along the way. I wrote the first half of this book, Chapters 1 and 2, in the winter of 2021–22 and most of the introduction the following summer. None of this writing has previously been published. Chapters 3, 4, and 5 appeared in somewhat different forms in 2020, 2014, and 2019 – bringing new material (biblical Eve, the concept of moral injury, three films written and directed by men working in the mainstream) to bear on my thinking about silence and voice, initiation and resistance, gender and development, patriarchy and democracy.

The opening paragraph of the Introduction dates back further, to the beginning of the 1990s when I wrote about my experience of listening to Anita Hill. That moment in time remains fixed in my memory because it brought home the difference between having a voice and being heard. Nowadays I find myself skeptical when I hear people speak of finding their voice as though this in itself will solve the myriad problems, both psychological and political, that follow in the wake of discovering that one's experience cannot be heard, or will not be listened to and taken seriously. I recall being on a train in Japan, going from Kyoto to Tokyo. A graduate student had kindly offered to accompany me so I would not get lost in the Tokyo railway station. She was asking me about voice, about losing one's voice, and when I said that nobody loses their voice, her face brightened. Would I write this in her notebook? she asked, handing me the book. "Nobody loses their voice," I repeated as I inscribed the words on a blank page; people may silence their voice, I said, but it is always for a reason.

My deepest thanks to John Thompson, who embraced the idea of this book and brought his intelligence to bear in editing that was truly a gift. I am grateful to the three readers for Polity whose comments and suggestions I found exceptionally helpful. I owe an immense debt of gratitude for years of conversation to David Richards and to Niobe Way. To Naomi Snider, special thanks. To Judy Chu, Randy Testa, Walla Elshekh, Xanthia Hargreaves, Rachel Marandett, Amelia Spittal, and Briana Thomas. And to those writers who have been the best of friends – Jorie Graham, Rachel Kadish, Daphne Merkin, and Honor Moore. To Sarah Chalfant for her discerning ear and eye, and her wise suggestions. To Carol Brandt for the conversation in the coffee shop in Abu Dhabi. To Tina Packer, always. And to Jim, for listening, and then listening again.

The common humanity of people . . . is the only real protector of human rights.

Jan Karski

Introduction

In the Fall of 1991, the house across the street from mine was being painted, and the painters brought their radio to work each day, placing it alongside them on the scaffold. At the time, the United States Senate Judiciary Committee, acting under pressure, had called Professor Anita Hill to testify about the nomination of Clarence Thomas for Supreme Court Justice. The radio was turned up loud, and Anita Hill's voice was riveting. The calm, steady sound of her speaking flowed down the street like a river. And then her voice was filtered through the responses of the senators. I remember the two-step process of listening to Anita Hill – hearing her, and then hearing her not being heard.

At the time I began writing *In a Different Voice*, women's voices were conspicuously missing from the psychology I was teaching. Or rather, women's voices were inconspicuously missing. The inconspicuousness of an omission so huge as to be monumental – women are, after all, more than half the population – was, in part, what led me to write. But to be honest, what spurred me more was a growing awareness of how readily a woman would not be heard, or would be misunderstood, when she gave voice to what she knew on the basis of her own experience, or said what she really thought.

With "In a Different Voice," first the essay and then the book, I broke a silence. My silence. What I did not know at the time was that it wasn't just my silence. Writing about a different voice, I had set out to remove a filter that kept aspects of human experience undercover, so to speak. But hearing the response to Anita Hill's testimony, it was clear: that filter was still in place. Speaking was one thing, being heard was another. Anita Hill had spoken clearly, but what she said was not taken seriously.

Following the 2022 US Supreme Court's ruling in Dobbs *v.* Jackson Women's Health Organization, it became legal, or legal again, for a state to silence a woman, so that in effect she has no voice and no choice if she becomes pregnant. Disrupting any comfortable progress narrative about women or women's voices or about equal voice as the bedrock of democracy, the Court, by overturning Roe, has made the questions raised by *In a Different Voice* startlingly contemporary. In answer to the question "Why this book right now?" there is a relevant and poignant link between this moment and the time when I conducted the interviews that led to my discoveries. I will begin at the beginning.

The year is 1973. President Nixon has ended the Vietnam War draft and the Supreme Court ruling in Roe *v.* Wade has legalized abortion. I am teaching part time at Harvard. My PhD is in psychology, and, since receiving my degree in 1964, I have taught with Erik

Erikson and also with Lawrence Kohlberg. In fact, it was their work on identity and on morality – specifically, Erikson's insistence that you cannot take a life history out of history, that life history and history are intricately conjoined, and Kohlberg's conviction that after the Holocaust, a stance of value neutrality or cultural relativism was untenable for the social sciences – that inspired me and drew me back into the field of psychology. Still, I was the mother of three young children, a modern dancer, and active in the civil rights and antiwar movements. As an undergraduate at Swarthmore, I had majored in English literature, and perhaps it was this in part that spurred my interest in how people think about themselves and about morality when they are facing real situations of conflict and choice. I was interested in questions of identity and morality, or, as Larry Kohlberg put it at the time, in the relationship between judgment and action.

And so, noticing a reticence among the men in the discussion section of Kohlberg's course on moral and political choice, which I was leading – their outspokenness when it came to talking about the Vietnam War, which most considered unjust, but their silence when the subject became whether or not one should resist the draft, a choice that, upon graduation, many of them would face – I decided to follow these students and interview them when they were college seniors and the draft decision was upon them. And then President Nixon ended the draft.

So it was that the locus of my study shifted. I was looking for a situation where people have to make a choice, where issues of identity and morality are at stake, and where they will have to live with the consequences of their decision. Real versus hypothetical moral dilemmas. And the Supreme Court came to my aid. Roe *v.* Wade: 1973. My study would focus on abortion decisions, where people would come to a public place (pregnancy counseling clinics) and the decision would be made within a limited time frame. At the time, it didn't strike me that the participants in the draft decision study were men, and in the abortion decision study they were women. My interest was in identity and moral development.

Between 1973 and 1975, together with Mary Belenky, then a graduate student at Harvard and also my neighbor and friend, I interviewed twenty-nine women who were in the first trimester of a confirmed pregnancy and who were considering abortion. The women were referred to our study from store-front clinics in Boston's South End, from pregnancy counseling services (Preterm and Planned Parenthood), and from university counseling services. Some, teenagers especially, were referred by counselors who were concerned about repeated abortions; some came because they were unsure about what decision to make and welcomed the opportunity to talk; and some came because they wanted to contribute to research. The women ranged in age from 15 to 33 and were diverse in race, ethnicity, and social class. Of the twenty-nine women, four decided to have the baby, two miscarried, twenty-one chose to have an abortion, and two were undecided at the time of the interview and could not be contacted at the time of the follow-up study. Complete interview data were available for twenty-four of the women, and, of these, twenty-one were interviewed again at the end of the year following their decision.

Introduction

In the winter of 1975–76, my husband and I moved from one suburb of Boston to another. For our three children, it was like moving from one world to another, because for them it meant new schools, new friends, and a new neighborhood to get used to. I stayed home that year to help them adjust to the change. I had a small research stipend to support the abortion decision study and, during the days when the children were in school, I would read through the interviews that Mary and I had conducted.

It was during that winter, on a day that remains etched in my memory, that my friend Dora Ullian came over. She was a graduate student studying psychology at Harvard, also interested in moral development. We were in the kitchen where I had been reading through the interview transcripts and I said, you know, I understand why psychologists have so much trouble understanding women. At the time, I was teaching (and Dora was studying) the theories of Freud and Erikson, Piaget and Kohlberg, all of whom had confessed to being puzzled by women, whom they observed to be less developed than men both in their sense of self and in their capacity for moral judgment. According to Freud, women have less sense of justice than men. On Kohlberg's six-stage scale of moral development, women typically score at the third or interpersonal stage and are less likely than men to progress to the more abstract or principled stages of moral reasoning. According to Erikson, women fuse or confuse identity with intimacy, and Piaget observed that, in contrast to boys, girls give priority to relationships over rules.[1]

Reading through the interview transcripts, listening in particular for how the women speak about themselves and about morality, I heard a tendency to construct moral problems differently – to start as it were from a different place, that is, from an assumption of connectedness rather than separateness. I said some such thing to Dora and she said, "That's interesting, why don't you write about it?"

And that's the origin of *In a Different Voice*. The abortion decision study was the impetus for the article and the centerpiece of the book, the focus of its two central chapters: Chapter 3, "Concepts of Self and Morality," and Chapter 4, "Crisis and Transition."[2] Yet as far as I'm aware (my research here has been on Google), despite all the talk about *In a Different Voice*, there has been a radio silence around the abortion decision study. It's almost never mentioned, and, if mentioned, it's almost exclusively only by me.

The initial paper, which I wrote in the winter of 1975, circulated among my students who sent it to friends who sent it to friends. It was the time of purple mimeograph machines, and the essay circulated like *samizdat,* which fit with my sense of myself at the time as a member of some sort of underground. Then one day, one of these students, who was on the editorial board of the *Harvard Educational Review*, asked if he could submit the paper to the journal. And without thinking much about it, I said okay.

I don't remember how long they kept it. Only that it came back saying, "Rejected." Just that. No request to revise and resubmit. Just rejected. Along with the comment, "We don't know what this is."

And that got my back up. You don't know what this is? I will add headings. Which I did, and sent it back to them.

This time when the paper came back, they said, "This is not social science." They said if I would rewrite the paper in an impersonal voice and from an objective standpoint, they would consider it.

I said: "It's called 'In a Different Voice'."

And for whatever reason, I suspect because by that time they were tired of dealing with me, or perhaps it was my insistence on being heard, they decided to publish the paper and be done with it.

That the essay went on to become a citation classic, the best-selling reprint of the *Harvard Educational Review* and the centerpiece of my 1982 book, makes this a good story to tell to graduate students who are tempted to withdraw in the face of rejection, or cannot imagine that *In a Different Voice* could have had such an inauspicious beginning. But telling this story recently, on two occasions when I was asked to speak about my book, I came to see that at the very outset "In a Different Voice" was recognized for what it was: a disruption. We don't know what this is!

"But, you may say, . . .," Virginia Woolf begins in *A Room of One's Own*.[3] Before saying a word on her subject, she anticipates interruption. She knows she will not be speaking about women and fiction in the way that people expect. Thus, she feels compelled to start by addressing people's objections to what she will say.

bell hooks writes in a similar vein:

> I was never taught absolute silence. I was taught that it was important to speak but to talk a talk that was itself a silence. Taught to speak and beware of the betrayal of too much heard speech. I experienced intense confusion and deep anxiety in my efforts to speak and to write.[4]

Once I realized that, from the very outset, "In a Different Voice" was recognized as a disruption – I was disrupting the conversation about psychology and morality by asking people to listen to the voice of that conversation – I came to an insight that solved what previously had been a puzzle. I saw how the disruption had been smoothed over, made less disruptive – and here's the insight – because a problem in psychological and moral theory became a problem about women. Women. Oh, right, women. Women have always been a problem, but now we know that we should listen to women and include women in studies of human psychology because in fact women are humans – and so it goes on. All of which is true, but not really the point.

In a sleight of hand, "We don't know what this is" had become "We know what this is." "In a Different Voice" was about women and women's development, about women being different from men. The different voice was coopted, conscripted one might say; heard as "feminine," it was placed within the very framework or way of speaking about women and about morality that my focus on the idea of a *different voice* had challenged.

When a voice that protests and resists is silenced, the stage is set for a confusion of tongues, to borrow Ferenczi's phrase. As a psychoanalyst, Ferenczi observed how patients who have been abused in childhood may come to identify with the aggressor. Having experienced their own voice as ineffective, they will speak in the voice of the aggressor, confusing that voice with their own.[5]

In the years immediately following publication of *In a Different Voice*, I set out to study girls' development and also to clarify what I meant by a different voice and an ethic of care. Although both the different voice and caring sounded "feminine" and were associated with women, I was not an essentialist. Rather, the gendering of care and caring as "feminine," together with the fact that I heard the voice of care ethics as a feminine voice, alerted me to the construction of gender as a binary (either masculine or feminine) and a hierarchy (privileging the masculine). To Socrates and Freud, to Kohlberg and Piaget, and in moral theory more generally, virtue is one and its name is justice. Care is a "supererogatory" duty: good, but not morally required (except of course in the case of women). The gender binary and hierarchy were obvious.

It became essential then for me to address the confusion between what sounds or is considered feminine and women. As the philosopher Manon Garcia puts it in the title of her recent book, *We Are Not Born Submissive*, it is "patriarchy [that] shapes women's lives."[6]

In a study published in the *Merrill Palmer Quarterly* in 1988 ("Two Moral Orientations: Gender Differences and Similarities"), Jane Attanucci and I looked at the relationship between moral orientation and gender. Analyzing the responses of medical students to Kohlberg's hypothetical moral dilemmas, we found that the men divided 50/50 between those who oriented to justice only and those who introduced considerations of both justice and care into solving moral problems. With the women, a third considered justice only, a third spoke about both justice and care, and a third oriented to care only. Care is not essentially or exclusively a woman's concern, although, at least in this sample of medical students, concerns about care and caring were articulated more often by women, and only women responded to moral problems by speaking solely about care.[7]

In a book chapter published the previous year ("The Origins of Morality in Early Childhood Relationships"), Grant Wiggins and I had observed that concerns about oppression (using power unfairly) and concerns about abandonment (failing to care) are human concerns, built into the human life cycle.[8] Listening to children, one hears the appeal to morality in their cries, "It's not fair!" and "You don't care!"

It was the research with girls, however, that shifted the focus of my attention from elaborating and clarifying the different voice to asking what stands in the way of our seeing what is right in front of our eyes. And here, the construction of gender as a binary and a hierarchy came to the fore as the blind that keeps us from seeing and saying the obvious. Concerns about justice and concerns about care are human concerns.

In the resisting injustice seminar that I teach with David Richards at the NYU School of Law, in the week that we read *Meeting at the Crossroads*[9] – a five-year study of close to 100 girls between the ages of 7 and 18 – a law student reflects:

> Reading through the girls' responses and the research team's explanations, I could not help but feel that they were bringing to light a lot of the values and behaviors I was taught as a child, particularly the notion of a "good woman" or falling into the perfect girl model. I recall countless examples growing up of being told to be quiet, patient, and friendly, that confronting problems was terrible, and that it was better to avoid at all costs and allow moments of tension to pass by, continuing to act as if nothing happened at all.

She continues: "I remember a huge chunk of my life where my response to everything was 'I don't know,' and where I (still to this day) will preface my response with this phrase." Then, asking what this means in relation to resisting injustice, she makes a stunning observation: "When we teach people not to use their voices openly and authentically, we sew a veil of doubt over everything they know, which stifles their willingness to speak and confront conflict."

Studying girls' development in the context of a culture obsessed with gender, where toys, like clothes, are divided into aisles of pink and blue, I witnessed a process of initiation that had been mistaken for development. In moving from childhood into adolescence and becoming, in the eyes of the world, young women, in entering secondary education and learning how to think about thinking, girls come under pressure to divide their minds from their (female) bodies, their thoughts from their emotions, and themselves – their honest voices – from their relationships. The initiation is scripted by gender. Its codes and scripts of manhood and womanhood follow the binary and the hierarchy. Morality comes into play in the sense that children must learn not only what they need to do but also what they "should" do – what is the right thing to do – if they want to establish themselves and be perceived by others as a "real boy" or a "good girl." In their desire to be included and for the sake of gaining respect and making their way in a world that is preoccupied with gender, children will divorce their sense of themselves from those aspects of themselves that might lead their masculinity or their femininity to be called into question. And in the course of secondary education, they will learn how to speak about love and truth and reality and morality. That is, they will learn what they can and cannot say if they want to be with others and they want others to want to be with them. They will learn what is and is not taken to be knowledge.

This initiation of children into the gender codes and scripts that undergird a patriarchal world, a world that privileges the voices of fathers – where a father's voice is the voice of morality and law – is marked by a change in voice. This change in voice reflects a loss of resonance, which in turn reflects a loss of relationship. Paradoxically, children are required to sacrifice relationship – their desire to live in connection with themselves and with others – in order to have "relationships." To have "relationships," children must learn to hold back parts of themselves from relationship, as a girl's honest voice comes to sound "stupid" or "rude" or "crazy," and a boy's emotionally open voice is heard as "babyish" or "girly" or "gay."

Across a diversity of race, ethnicity, and social class, shrewd and feisty girls named what they recognized to be a crisis of connection. They were describing a predicament that is truly a predicament. If they said what they were feeling and thinking, no one would want to be with them. "My voice would be too loud," one girl explained. But if they don't say what they are feeling and thinking, then still no one will be with them. They will be all alone. Either way – by speaking honestly or not speaking honestly – they will lose relationship. In coming of age, girls were being initiated into a kind of silence.[10]

The crisis of connection that articulate girls named was then identified by Niobe Way as one of the "deep secrets" of boys' development.[11] For boys as for girls, a loss that was felt was said to be not a loss but a gain. A sacrifice of relationship was seemingly the price one pays for having relationships, built into the nature of things, a necessary loss, part of what it means to grow up. A force in the world was thus sowing confusion, complicating children's ability to trust their feelings, or to see what they had lost as something of value.

In the 1990s, the neurobiologist Antonio Damasio had a growing realization of error. On the basis of research evidence, he recognized that the separation of thought from emotion, long taken as a milestone of cognitive development, the *sine qua non* of rationality, was a manifestation of brain injury or trauma.[12] Psychologists studying development had reached a similar conclusion: the separation of the self from relationships was, rather than a sign of maturation, a residue of trauma – a response to the experience of having been overwhelmed.[13]

In 1996, roughly twenty years after I first wrote about a "different voice," I wrote the word "patriarchy." It was in a chapter for a book on the proceedings of the annual Piaget Society Symposium. A puzzle had come to my attention. In the mid-nineteenth century, a psychiatrist observed that girls are more liable to suffer at adolescence. Anyone who works in schools knows that, prior to adolescence, boys are more prone to psychological difficulties, more likely to show signs of depression along with learning and attention disorders, speech and behavior problems, whereas for girls, adolescence marks a sudden high incidence of depression, eating disorders, cutting, and other forms of destructive behavior. Yet this striking gender disparity – this difference between boys and girls with respect to the times when their resilience is at heightened risk – although observed for over a century, remained unexplained and unexplored.

I titled my chapter, "The Centrality of Relationship in Human Development" – by now you can see the direction of my thinking. My subtitle was: "A puzzle, some evidence, and a theory." The puzzle was the gender disparity, the evidence came from the studies with girls that had illuminated a process of initiation. The theory was that children's initiation into the gender binaries and hierarchies of patriarchy poses a risk to their resilience and thus is marked by signs of psychological distress. The earlier timing of boys' initiation (roughly between the ages of 4 and 7) compared to the later initiation of girls (which typically occurs at adolescence) explains the gender disparity.[14]

In his studies of depression, Martin Seligman had called attention to a "flip-flop" in the rates of depression, with boys showing more signs of depression than girls up until adolescence when the flip-flop occurs. Observing that, whatever causes this shift in the rates of depression by gender, it doesn't have its roots in girls' childhood, Seligman concluded that something must happen to girls at adolescence.[15]

Girls' resistance provided the clue. Girls were resisting the strictures of patriarchy, the gender binary that would have them split their thoughts from their emotions, their minds from their bodies, and themselves – the voice that says what they are feeling and thinking – from their relationships. And also the hierarchy that renders them submissive to the voices of fathers, heard as the voice of authority. Girls were resisting letting go of the way they saw things and silencing the voice that spoke from their own experience – the voice that said what they knew first hand.

It was from girls that I first learned about initiation and about resistance. Women will shudder at the mention of 7th grade, recalling the cliques, the exclusion, and also the so-called "perfect girl" who, by her seeming existence, renders all other girls imperfect. Something was driving these divisions among girls, and, as Seligman suspected, it was not rooted in their childhood. As Maxine Hong Kingston observes in her coming-of-age novel, *The Woman Warrior,* it wasn't just *her* family.[16] A force in the world was impinging on girls when they reached adolescence.

The studies with girls thus brought the account of psychological development into the political arena. Articulate girls had named a crisis of connection: a turning point where what once had seemed ordinary – having a voice and living in relationships – became extraordinary.[17] An initiation that was culturally sanctioned and socially enforced had led, in Ferenczi's terms, to a confusion of tongues, where the voice of experience was seemingly lost or discredited, displaced by a voice that was heard as carrying more authority and was mistaken for one's own. Children's initiation into the gender codes and scripts of a patriarchal order of living bore some of the hallmarks of trauma.

By this time, the word "patriarchy" had taken on a very specific meaning for me. Put simply, patriarchy is an order of living based on a gender binary and hierarchy. To be a man, one must be masculine, not feminine, and also superior – both to men who are not perceived as real men and to women. In patriarchy, the order is: him over her, straight over gay.

The cardinal discovery of the studies of development that began with girls in the 1980s and then continued with boys in the 1990s and into the twenty-first century lay in the realization that the gender binaries and hierarchies of a patriarchal order compromise basic human relational capacities.[18] By splitting reason (masculine) from emotion (feminine), the mind from the body, and the self from relationships, the binaries undercut our ability to think about what we are feeling, to know what is happening in our body, to stay in touch with other people, and thus to navigate the human social world. By doing so, they set the stage for and justify the hierarchy that privileges the masculine over the feminine (reason over emotion, the self over relationships, justice over caring). At once idealized and devalued, the feminine falls, in effect, off the map of human experience. The Build Back Better Act that the US Congress passed in November 2021 contained no funds for childcare. In fact, it was the elimination of funds for care work that secured the passage of the bill.

By undercutting human relational capabilities, the initiation into patriarchy compromises children's ability to survive and to thrive. It also lays the ground for all forms of oppression, whether on the basis of race, class, caste, sexuality, religion, or what have you. This is because children's internalization of gender codes, which require them to dissociate themselves from aspects of their humanity, clouds their ability to perceive and to resist injustice.[19]

To put it starkly, like a healthy body that resists infection, so a healthy psyche resists the culture of patriarchy – because its gender binaries and hierarchies compromise the relational capabilities that we rely on in order to survive and to thrive.[20]

What at first glance had presented as a problem with women, or a women's problem, proved on close listening

– over time and with increasing knowledge – to be a human problem. Like canaries in mines, girls coming of age were signaling a danger to human survival.

"In a Different Voice" was the first thing I wrote for myself. With the resonance of other women's voices – the women who took part in my studies and my women friends and also the women's movement, the voices of second-wave feminism – I said what I really thought about women and moral development and the psychology I was teaching.

The secret at the heart of my work, which for a long time I couldn't quite find a way to articulate or say clearly, is that although gender is central to the story I tell, it is not a story about gender. It is a human story. And so, I have changed my title.

This book records an experience of reaching a clarity that took place over a number of years. With the force of an epiphany, I realized that where I had been taught to see development, I was witnessing initiation and resistance. What was at stake was the capacity to care. "So obvious that no one noticed," as the narrator comments in Arundhati Roy's novel *The God of Small Things*.[21]

In the transcripts of research interviews with girls, the phrase "I don't know" marked this rite of passage in girls' lives. An injunction – "don't" – had come between "I" and "know." In her studies of adolescent boys' friendships, Niobe Way heard a comparable phrase, "I don't care," which marked boys' passage into manhood. A kind of psychological denial, a dissociation of the self, the "I," from knowing or from caring was required for children to establish themselves and be perceived by others as good women, or real men. So that in effect women were to care without knowing and men were to know without caring. Meaning that none of it made sense.

The research on development that began in the 1980s and '90s thus showed patriarchy to rest on a shaky psychological foundation, vulnerable to women knowing and men caring and contingent on everyone forgetting what they had once cared about and known. Because patriarchy is not natural, as Naomi Snider and I point out in asking *Why Does Patriarchy Persist?*, because humans are relational beings, born with a voice and with the desire to live not alone but in relationships, because, as the evolutionary anthropologist Sarah Blaffer Hrdy observes, "patriarchal ideologies that focused on both the chastity of women and the perpetuation and augmentation of male lineages undercut the long-standing priority of putting children's well-being first,"[22] patriarchy depends for its continuation on violence and on silence. Male violence or the threat of male violence holds its hierarchy of male privilege and power in place and women's silence keeps its secrets. Rather than being linked with human survival, patriarchy puts our survival in danger.

In the years when I taught with Erik Erikson, he would say that if you want to know which issue the culture has not resolved, pay attention to the adolescents. They will put their finger on it and dramatize the problem. So it is today with pronouns. Whatever one thinks about "they" or "zee" or other nonbinary alternatives to he/she, they have a point. For the adolescents, as Erikson would remind us, it's a matter of identity.

The way I have come to see it, the tension between constructing gender as a binary and a hierarchy and

seeing gender as fluid, or a spectrum, is the difference between patriarchy and democracy. In patriarchy,
gender is essential; in democracy, gender is irrelevant.
Democracy rests on a commitment to equal voice, which
is the condition for resolving conflicts in relationship,
through open discussion and debate rather than through
the use of force. It is in this respect, with regard to voice
and violence, or voting versus violence, that democracy
and patriarchy are opposites.

The Supreme Court decision in Dobbs *v.* Jackson
brings all this home. To say it plainly, in the United
States in the twenty-first century, a patriarchal voice has
been reinstated as the voice of morality and law, and
selflessness has been restored as the criterion for judging
who is and who is not a good woman.

To read *In a Different Voice* now, then, means
revisiting in this light the insight that several women
in the abortion decision study came to: namely, that
selflessness, long considered the epitome of feminine
goodness, is in fact morally problematic. My hunch is
that this is one reason the abortion study is not talked
about. Because it is precisely this that is most contentious: the claim of women to have a voice, along with
the recognition that having a voice is integral to rather
than antithetical to caring. Because to care, to do the
work of caring, it is necessary to be present, to be in
relationship, and to pay attention. For a woman to
render herself "selfless" – seemingly without a voice or
needs or perceptions of her own – rather than signifying goodness is an act of abdication. An abdication of
voice and an evasion of responsibility and relationship.
The Court's decision in Roe had cut the ground away
from under what had been the moral justification for

women's silence. Selflessness, which had been valorized in the name of care and caring, was in fact careless. Carelessness masquerading under the guise of goodness.

In the week that we read *Meeting at the Crossroads* in the resisting injustice seminar, a law student reflects on a silence that she has become curious about:

> In many ways these years following my high school graduation were a period of unlearning and recovering from what was, in many ways, the trauma of my childhood educational experience. I was able to find a voice – one that I am quite proud of – but I almost never talk about my childhood schooling. And I certainly do not think that's a coincidence. I even struggled with deciding if I was comfortable writing this short, inherently broad response paper about it because I still don't think I have processed it enough to do so. Now, I engage in resistance work essentially every day but I find that I avoid work that even remotely touches on gender. In essence, I avoid anything that would force me to reflect on my childhood.

Among the girls' voices that Lyn Mikel Brown and I record in our book, 11-year-old Jessie's voice is the one that stays with this law student. Quoting from *Crossroads*, she is struck by the observation that Jessie

> with age "is more subtle, cognitively more sophisticated in her understanding of herself and the social world," but also is "more willing to forget what really happened or to say that what she knows through experience probably didn't happen, than to feel out of touch with what others say is reality."[23]

She reflects that, like Jessie, she is also more willing to forget what really happened – more willing to say that what she knows through experience probably didn't happen – than to feel out of touch with what others say is reality. In her eyes, this was the trauma of her education. I am struck by her candor and the courage of her admission: although she engages in resistance work essentially every day, she avoids work "that even remotely touches on gender." As a student in the resisting injustice seminar, she is now asking herself: How come?

It is a truism of trauma studies, as Judith Herman reminds us, that the perpetrator depends on the bystander to do nothing.[24] So we come to forget – and seemingly not to know what within ourselves we know, or not to care about what in truth we care about. To say it another way, with the initiation into the gender codes and scripts of patriarchy, we become unreliable narrators of our own life stories.

On the last day of the term in my seminar on listening, a student sent me an email. She was grateful for the class, for its focus on listening and on being curious. "Most of all," she writes, she wanted me to know how grateful she was that I had "responded with disbelief" when, in her presentation to the class that day, she had questioned the meaning of the word "dissociative" and said that she didn't know what it was doing in the transcript of the interview she had conducted. "Dissociative" had been used twice by the person she interviewed.

Listening to her presentation, taking in her observation that in the interview "*I don't know* is everywhere," it was clear to me that in fact she knew what "dissociative" was doing on this psychological landscape and also what it meant. In truth, it spoke directly to her question as to how women can emotionally stomach doing sex work.

"It has been really eye-opening," the student continued, "to practice listening to myself, and to what I already know." My breathing slowed as I took in what followed: "I find too often, in various parts of my life, I have not trusted my own intuition, or stopped short of coming to conclusions that I have the evidence for, and haven't known why."

A former litigator, now studying for a master's degree in law, she had written to thank me for "giving me and our class the permission to listen to and impart this trust in ourselves – it means so much to me, more than you may have been aware of."

It is easy for me to forget. Or to think that this problem of women needing permission to listen to themselves, or to trust conclusions that they have the evidence for, is a thing of the past. The student is white, and I find myself wondering if this is especially true for white women, who, on the basis of race, can have the illusion of inclusion.

I reread the email – "[I have] stopped short of coming to conclusions that I have the evidence for, and haven't known why." I am moved by her honesty, by the specificity of her self-awareness, the precision of her observation: even when she has the evidence, she stops short, and she doesn't know why. What if she didn't stop short, I find myself wondering? What does she imagine would happen? And in fact, what might happen then?

It was adolescent girls who taught me to listen for the words "really" and "actually" and to hear how they can signal a switch from saying what I think to saying what I really think, or how I actually feel. It was girls coming of age who showed me how a human voice goes undercover – how "I don't know" can become a cover for "I know." In asking "How come?" – what stops a woman from trusting her intuition, or from drawing conclusions even when she has the evidence upon which to base them, or from saying what she really thinks or how she actually feels, what leads her to keep an honest voice undercover? – I found that in order to answer these questions I had to join a psychological explanation with a political understanding. Otherwise, I couldn't make sense of the evidence. Or explain the resistance, both the resistance of girls and also the resistance to what the studies with girls were uncovering.

My ears now prick up at the phrase "to be honest." Is it a prelude to a change in voice? A move into relationship? So that rather than saying what I say, I'll say what I would say if I were to be honest. I find myself wondering at what level of consciousness people are aware of making this shift, and also what prompts someone to do so.

These questions feel prescient at the present moment, when carelessness and indifference carry such risk. To hear the different voice, the voice of care ethics, for what it is: a human voice; to recognize that the voice it differs from is a patriarchal voice (bound to gender binaries and hierarchies); and to realize that where patriarchy is in force and enforced, the human voice is a voice of resistance

What this gives us is a place to begin.

1

Women's Voices and Women's Silences

On a Sunday in late November of 2021, *The New York Times* published a review of a book called *The Trouble with White Women*. Joan Morgan, the reviewer, began:

> To fully grasp the significance of Kyla Schuller's *The Trouble with White Women*, it helps to understand the feminist climate in which it arrives. There was Hillary Clinton's defeat in the 2016 presidential election, significantly abetted by the approximately 50 percent of white women who voted for Donald Trump; and then the US Supreme Court's refusal to block the law that bans abortions after six weeks of pregnancy. (A majority of white women in Texas voted for Gov. Greg Abbot and Senator Ted Cruz, both vocal supporters of that law.)[1]

There is no way of talking about women's voices in today's political climate without also talking about race. This means talking about the voices of the white women who abetted the defeat of Hillary Clinton and voted for the Texas politicians who supported the law to ban abortions beyond six weeks of pregnancy, as well as the voices of the white women who voted for Clinton and against the politicians who would ban abortion. It means talking about the voices of the 91 percent of Black women who voted for Clinton in 2016, and the 95 percent of Black women who voted for Joe Biden in 2020, and also those of the 53 percent of white women who, in 2020, voted to re-elect Donald Trump (Pew Research Foundation).[2] In short, it means talking about race and gender, asking why those Black women who voted voted overwhelmingly Democratic, more than any other group including Black men, and why a majority of white women who voted, as far as one can see, chose white supremacy over gender solidarity by voting for Trump in both the 2016 and the 2020 elections.

All of which is to say that my story about women's voices cannot be simply a story about gender. What's more, it is not about women versus men, as the gender binary would have it; or about women's oppression or submission within a gender hierarchy that privileges men. Instead, it is a story about resistance – one that includes Black people and white people, Black women and white women. Above all, it is a story about girls.

I wonder if you, dear reader, are struck by what I find so striking: girls in our midst who are giving voice to resistance. In some ways, we've always known this about girls. One has only to read Euripides' tragedy *Iphigenia in Aulis* to hear the voice of a daughter, Iphigenia, who, upon being summoned by her father Agamemnon and learning that he is preparing to sacrifice her in order to gain the winds that will carry the Greek army to Troy, tells him he is mad. Life without honor, she says, is preferable to death. Needless to say, he doesn't listen. She is countering the culture that he is defending, a culture that values honor over life.

In her second speech, after realizing that her voice has had no effect, Iphigenia dissuades her mother from protesting, explaining that she wants to be her father's sacrifice and to go down in history as the person responsible for restoring Greek honor.[3] It's a snapshot of initiation: the psyche aligning itself with the values of the culture in which it exists. To Aristotle, however, it is a flaw in playwriting because to him the change in voice is unexplained.[4]

Having spent ten years listening to girls at the very time of their initiation into a culture that values honor over life and privileges the voices of fathers, I can explain it. What's more, I heard this shift in voice over and over again among the girls I was studying, and witnessed the rewards that come to girls who align their voices with patriarchal norms and values. But I also witnessed girls' resistance to making this alliance and the effects of their resistance on women, and herein lies the story I want to tell: how women's voices and women's silences give us insights into understanding what otherwise is a puzzle in human development: why we accommodate to a culture that compromises our humanity. Because, as we have seen in our own time, girls' voices can be radically disruptive, especially when they are listened to.

I'm thinking of Greta Thunberg – "Don't thank me, do something," Greta told the members of Congress who rushed forward to thank her when she visited the US Capitol. Greta, whose one-person school strike when she was 15 – just Greta and her handwritten sign in front of the Swedish parliament – had, within sixteen months, inspired the largest climate demonstration in history: more than 4 million people from 161 countries joined the global climate strike on September 20, 2019. Greta, who became *Time* magazine's person of the year in 2019 and was nominated for the Nobel peace prize.

She's one. But here's another: Darnella Frazier. Of all the people who witnessed the murder of George Floyd by the policeman Derek Chauvin, Darnella, age 17, was the only one who took out her cell phone and clicked on the camera and recorded it. Filmed the entire incident, the close to ten minutes that Derek Chauvin kept his knee pressed on George Floyd's neck until he was dead. To the reporter who asked why she had filmed it, Darnella explained: "It wasn't right. He was suffering. He was in pain . . . The world needed to see what I was seeing." And because she filmed it, a white policeman, Derek Chauvin, was convicted of murdering a Black man, George Floyd. Her film was the evidence that proved crucial at the trial. As Darnella explained, "I opened my phone and started recording because I knew if I didn't no one would believe me."[5]

Why teenage girls? From a psychologist's vantage point, the more pressing question may be "What happened to everyone else?" How come the rest of the people who saw what was happening to George Floyd right in front of their eyes and heard his cries didn't take out their phones and record what clearly was not right? What about all the people for whom thanks from members of Congress would have sufficed, and who, unlike Greta, would not have pushed back with, "This is all wrong," or "How dare you?" – by which she meant, how dare you not act when my future is at stake?[6]

In 1981, after completing *In a Different Voice,* I learned, in the words of Joseph Adelson, editor of the

1980 *Handbook of Adolescent Psychology*, that adolescent girls had "simply not been much studied." The psychology of adolescence was "the study of the male youngster writ large."[7]

So be it, I thought, because this was true at the time of much of psychology, not to mention medical research where the signs of women's heart attacks are still described as "atypical," meaning not like men's. But ... in a book filled with women's voices – I'm speaking about *In a Different Voice*, where the two central chapters are about women who, in the immediate aftermath of Roe *v*. Wade, were pregnant and thinking about whether to continue or to abort the pregnancy – the single voice that many women readers found most unsettling was that of an 11-year-old girl, Amy, one of the two girls quoted in the book and the only girl quoted at any length. Maybe it was Amy's voice lingering in my mind along with the awareness that, even though I had been taught to hear her moral reasoning as "naive" and "wishy-washy," what she said made sense. Or maybe it was simply that I had just finished a book and, when the newly appointed principal of an all-girls' school approached me with a request to study girls because he could not find any research on girls' development, and he had raised the funds that would support my graduate students, I thought "why not?" What I remember from that time was going to the school to talk to the students about the study and one of the girls raising her hand and asking me: "What could you possibly learn by studying us?"

As it turned out, the studies with girls that began at Emma Willard in the early 1980s, and continued over a period of ten years in a range of public and private schools, girls' schools and coed schools, and after-school settings, turned out to be the most deeply illuminating work I have done.[8] And to me as well, that came as a surprise. Listening to girls in the years just before adolescence, I heard a voice that I knew and had forgotten, a voice that sounded at once familiar and surprising, and this in turn led me to realize that at a certain point in development, we are pressed to rewrite our history – to tell a story that is not quite our story, to replace one voice with another that then serves as a cover.

Studying girls, I became a witness to dissociation – a not knowing that was culturally inscribed and socially enforced. What I had learned to think of as steps in a developmental progression – the separation of reason from emotion, of the mind from the body, and the self from relationships – milestones on the march toward rationality, autonomy, and maturity, held this not knowing in place. Because if we cannot think about what we are feeling, if our mind doesn't register what is going on in our body, and if our self becomes like a mighty fortress, defended and boundaried rather than open and engaged in relationships, then we cannot know what otherwise we would know. Because it is only when our thoughts and our emotions are connected, when our minds and our bodies are joined, and when we are living in relationship with others rather than standing apart from them, that we can make sense of the human world.

Healthy children resist losing their embodied minds, their emotional intelligence, and their relational selves. But this healthy resistance brings them into conflict with a culture that valorizes separation and has enshrined a gender binary and hierarchy as the way things are and the way things have to be. That is, a healthy resistance brings children into conflict with the culture of patriarchy, where women seemingly lose their voices and men appear emotionally clueless, and people shrug, rather than asking: what has happened to this human being?

Following girls' development through the years of middle childhood and into adolescence, I saw a healthy resistance to losing voice and relationship become a political resistance, with girls speaking truth to power – think of Greta and Darnella, or for that matter 15-year-old Claudette Colvin who, claiming her constitutional right, was the first to refuse to give up her seat to a white woman on a crowded, segregated bus in Montgomery, Alabama. Colvin was arrested in March 1955, nine months before Rosa Parks refused to move to the back of the bus and became the icon of resistance to bus segregation.[9]

I also saw how girls' political resistance or truth-speaking comes under pressure and can go undercover or turn into what psychotherapists call a psychological resistance: a reluctance to know what one knows. I witnessed girls begin to not know what they knew and to cover the voice of their experience with a voice that carried more authority in the world around them. And I saw how, by doing so, they gained credibility in the eyes of the world, albeit at both a psychological and a political cost.

When the ten-year Harvard Project connecting women's psychology with girls' development expanded to include a study of young boys and their fathers, Judy Chu zeroed in on the time when boys start school and encounter pressure to establish themselves as a "real boy," or one of the boys. This is the time *When Boys Become Boys*, the title of Chu's 2014 book. By following a group of 4- and 5-year-olds as they move from prekindergarten through kindergarten and into first grade, Chu saw children who had been attentive, articulate, authentic, and direct in their relationships with one another and with her gradually becoming more inarticulate, more inattentive, more inauthentic, and indirect with one another and with her. They were becoming "boys," or how boys are often said to be. But, as Chu cautions, boys know more than they show.[10]

Chu was tracking a process of initiation whereby children, in their desire to establish themselves as boys, were putting on a cloak of masculinity. They were disguising themselves by shielding those aspects of themselves that would lead them to be seen as not masculine (meaning feminine) or as like a woman (girly or gay), in a world where being a man means being superior. Winners not losers, to quote our former president.

A picture was settling into place of an initiation that begins with young boys, roughly between the ages of 4 and 7, continues with girls when they reach adolescence (roughly between 11 and 14), and then replays with boys in the late years of high school, when, in the words of one of the boys in Way's studies, they "know how to be more of a man."[11] An initiation that mandates dissociation and compromises children's relational capacities – an initiation that leaves a psychological scar.

Which brings me then to what I see as a moment of opportunity, an opening that shows us a way to move forward. Three signposts, recently put into place, point a direction to follow: first to the need for radical listening, second to the lens of resistance and accommodation, and third to the tale of the emperor's new clothes, reminding us that we have the ability to break through dissociation and indoctrination, to see and to say what is happening right in front of our eyes. With these in mind, I will return at the end to girls' voices and women's silences and take up what now seems to me most pressing: how is it that we can come not to see the obvious, how can we come not to say or even know what in another sense we know? How do we come to betray what's right? Because although girls and women have been the focus of my attention, the "we" I refer to are human beings.

1. Radical Listening

The word radical means "root" and radical listening is a way of listening that gets to the root of what is being said and also what is not being said. It specifies a way of tuning in to the under-voice, the conversation beneath the conversation. Radical listening holds a potential for transformation because it starts from a place of not knowing and develops the muscle of curiosity.

As a practice of listening, radical listening begins with asking a real question – something you don't know and want to know. It hinges on replacing judgment with curiosity. Notice what happens, I tell my students, when you replace judgment with curiosity. Like asking real questions, replacing judgment with curiosity is harder than it sounds.[12]

In my early days of doing research on moral development, I was alerted to the need for radical listening by a woman whom I was interviewing. I had presented her with one of the dilemmas psychologists use to assess a person's stage of moral reasoning, and had posed the standard question: "What should Heinz do?" As

I recall, the woman was roughly my age and she hesitated, looking at me steadily. "Would you like to know what I think?" she asked. "Or would you like to know what I really think?"

Whatever prompted her to ask me that question, she was telling me that she had learned to think about morality in a way that differed from how she really thought. What's more, she was aware of the difference. She could tell me what she thinks about morality, or she could tell me what she really thinks, depending on what I would like to know. She was teaching me about initiation and also about resistance. But she was also cueing me to the need for a radical practice of listening, where one listens both for an initiated voice and for a voice that resists initiation – the voice of what I really think.

A change of voice, a change of heart. It was this change that I would see some girls resisting, loath to silence the voice that said what they "really" thought or felt. Reluctant to cover the voice that gave voice to their experience with a voice that said what others wanted to hear or expected them to say, or thought they should think and feel, and say and know, including about morality and about themselves.

"What do people say about you?" With my colleagues I had organized a weekly afterschool theater, writing, and outing club for girls.[13] We began with 9- and 10-year-olds, a time when girls' voices tend to be strong, when for the most part girls are outspoken and, in the presence of someone who listens, will say what they feel and think. The afterschool club was part of a three-year developmental study and intervention project designed to strengthen healthy resistance and courage in girls. In the final year of the project, when the girls were turning 12 and 13, they insisted, to my colleagues' and my dismay, on organizing a beauty contest. Yet having agreed that we would take turns with them in choosing our activities, we felt we couldn't say no. I recall watching girl after girl walk across the stage of the school auditorium where we were meeting that day. "What do people say about you?" each one was asked by another of the girls. The girls' attention was being directed outwards – to what people said about them, how they looked in the eyes of others. They were being initiated into what they would need to know in order to live as women in a society that was in transition yet still recognizably patriarchal.

Interviewing girls at this time, I found myself asking questions I had been taught never to ask; questions that would be considered "leading." And yet my questions proved key to a process of discovery that was unfolding before my eyes. "Is that true?" I would ask a girl who said something that struck me as inane, a mindless repetition of some cultural bromide or stereotype. "Do you really feel that way?" I asked a 16-year-old who had said she didn't like herself enough to look out for herself. In response, she told me how she "actually" looked out for herself: by never saying what she was really feeling and thinking. "Brilliant, isn't it?" she asked and I agreed. It was a brilliant strategy, in that she could dismiss whatever people might say about her, knowing that they had no idea who she was. But at the cost of what she had said she wanted: namely, honesty in relationships. In essence, she was looking out for herself at the cost of betraying herself.

"Do you really believe that?" I asked when a girl said something that struck me as banal or outlandish.

And perhaps it was my use of the word "really" or simply my questioning a culture that had been taken for granted, or perhaps my questions conveyed that I was in fact listening to what they were saying and interested in what they really thought or knew, but in response to such questions, I would hear a girl's voice shift to a lower register or, in a conspiratorial tone, she would tell me how she really felt, how she actually looked out for herself, or what within herself, on the basis of her own experience, she knew to be true. I was astounded. This was all it took to break through a process of initiation that had led one voice to cover another: the voice of what I think covering the voice of what I really think. Radical listening means listening for the undervoice, tuning one's ear to the conversation under the conversation – what remains unspoken until someone asks the question, or questions the culture that has driven a voice into silence.

"If I were to be quite honest," Anne Frank writes toward the end of what turns out to be the final entry in her diary. "If I were to be quite honest, I must admit . . ." For years I have used this diary entry as a common text when I teach workshops or classes on the Listening Guide. But only in the past few years, as I have come to think more about radical listening, did I actually pay attention to what Anne was saying. "If I were to be quite honest, I must admit . . ." I had started tracking people's use of the words "actually," or "really," and found that they can signal a shift from an initiated voice – a voice constrained by the gender binary and hierarchy – to an uninitiated or wild voice: the voice that says what I feel and think. By taking what Anne said seriously, I saw that following her saying that if she were to be quite honest, she reframes what initially she had presented as the problem.

Anne begins her diary entry, dated August 1, 1944, by repeating what people have said about her – "little bundle of contradictions" she has been called, and she thinks the name fits. She is beset by contradictions both from without and from within. And yet, if she were to be quite honest, she must admit that rather than a problem of contradiction (from without and from within), the problem she faces is a problem of relationship. She can see no way to become "what I would so like to be and what I could be" and also be with other people living in the world. The relational impasse I heard girl after girl describe is named by Anne Frank. What in the eyes of the world appeared as a problem with herself ("little bundle of contradictions") was in truth a seemingly insoluble problem of relationship. Anne could see no way to be herself and also be with other people, given the world she was living in.[14]

2. The lens of resistance and accommodation

In an article published in *Child Development Perspectives* in the winter of 2021, Leoandra Onnie Rogers and Niobe Way observe that it is impossible any longer to talk about child development without situating it in and in response to the ideological context. This means viewing children's development through the lens of resistance and accommodation. "Every aspect of child development – from cognition to relationships – is shaped by macrolevel ideologies (e.g. white supremacy, patriarchy) that reflect the social hierarchies and embedded power structures of society." Rather than focusing on adjustment, it is necessary to "direct the field's attention away from 'fixing' individuals and microsystems and toward disrupting the macro-ideologies that shape them." Thus, Rogers and Way ground their approach in research on resistance and accommodation to such ideologies – research that reveals that "as humans we have a natural capacity to resist what gets in the way of our ability to survive and thrive."[15]

But as we also know, resistance has its costs. In *We Are Not Born Submissive*, Manon Garcia challenges the view that women are either submissive by nature or lack moral agency.[16] Instead, she writes, women's submission may reflect a keen assessment as to the costs of freedom. Rather than signifying her essential nature or a failure of moral agency, a woman's submission to the constraints of a patriarchal order may reflect a shrewd cost-benefit analysis on her part concerning the price she will pay for freedom.

One has only to recall how Elizabeth Warren, once held up as the woman whom women would vote for (in contrast to Hillary Clinton), when she was actually running for president was described in precisely the same unflattering terms that had been used to denigrate Clinton. Warren, it turned out, was also not the right woman to run for president, leading to the suspicion that perhaps no woman who actually runs for president could be the right person for that position.

3. The tale of the emperor's new clothes

In a paper presented at the conference "Patriarchy and its Discontents: The Fierce Urgency of Now," sponsored by the William Alanson White Institute in

November 2020, Naomi Snider takes on the question of masks and unmasking.[17] In her talk, titled "Unmasking Psychoanalysis: An Emperor, a Boy, and the Search for New Clothes," Snider, who is white, begins by quoting the Black psychoanalyst Beverly Stout on the subject of racism. Stout had diagnosed psychoanalysis's neglect of American racism not as a blind spot – because it was right there in plain sight – but as "racial agnosia," from the term visual agnosia, an impairment in recognition of visually presented objects. Racial agnosia, Stout said, is "a defense against seeing what is obvious."

It was a short step, Snider discovered, from racial agnosia to the tale of "a willfully oblivious emperor, a child who dares to say what he sees – and my own search for a new set of analytic clothes."

Snider, formerly my student, my co-author in *Why Does Patriarchy Persist?*, and a human rights lawyer who has become a psychoanalyst, reminds us of a story about

> an emperor who for his birthday was to have a large parade where all the townspeople would gather to celebrate his majesty. He employed two weavers who promised clothes so fine and wonderful that only the great and good in society would be able to see them. The clothes, they said, would be quite invisible to anyone who is stupid, incompetent, or unworthy. On the day of the celebration, as the emperor walked the streets, his subjects gathered enraptured by his wondrous gowns. Never before had anyone seen such splendor the townsfolk all cried. All, that is, except one small boy – who saw what was right in front of his eyes and simply said what he saw. "The emperor is naked," he exclaimed.

Snider reflects:

> I – perhaps like many others drawn to the psychoanalytic field – have often felt like the child in this story – able to see what others won't acknowledge. Perhaps this is why this story has stayed with me – as a sort of parable of the costs that come with speaking your mind. For in my meme story, no good came of the boy's revelation: the emperor was shamed, and the boy was ignored – ridiculed and shunned. Everyone would have been much happier had he simply stayed quiet. And so, while I have often felt like the boy in the story, I have learned to become like the townsfolk – to see what I am supposed to see, to say what others want me to say, and to otherwise keep my mouth shut.
>
> In later years, as I learned the word patriarchy, the folktale took on deeper and more political layers. A story about a naked emperor who covers himself in the pretense of gowns and grandeur became a metaphor for the empty lie of male superiority upon which patriarchal authority depends, and the blind complicity that sustains it.

All well and good, except that's not how the story ends. What's more, as Snider sees:

> in the young boy who simply says what he sees, Andersen captures – as so many artists have done – the inherent knowing of children, and with it their ability to pierce the veil of patriarchal masculinity and femininity and challenge the authority of the patriarchal father and his claims to privileged knowledge.

She is referring to the relational knowing of 4-year-old Jake, who says to his mother, "You have a happy voice, but I also hear a little worried voice," of Dan who remembers that, when he was a young boy, he and his mother were pals. Recalling the afternoons they spent in the kitchen baking together, Dan says, "I saw the face behind her face, and she was angry." Dan knew that his mother did not want people to see what he saw.

This emotionally astute and honest voice is the voice of the 5-year-old who asks his mother, "Mama, why do you smile when you're sad?," the voice of the 5-year-old who tells his father, "You are afraid that if you hit me, when I grow up I'll hit my children," the voice of 11-year-old Elise who, in a conversation about whether it is ever good to lie, says "My house is wallpapered with lies." Like the small boy in Andersen's tale, these children give voice to what it has taken centuries for the human sciences to acknowledge: the human world is far more transparent than is commonly assumed. In essence, we learn *not* to see what is right in front of our eyes, *not* to know what in another sense is obvious.

Across the human sciences, a growing consensus now recognizes empathy as an age-old human capacity; we come into this world equipped with mirror neurons. Sarah Blaffer Hrdy directs our attention to "the evolutionary origins of mutual understanding" by underscoring the long interval for humans between birth and reproductive maturity. Evolution selected for "empathy, mind-reading, and cooperation" because the ability to engage others and elicit care was essential to our survival as a species.[18]

In recent years it has become increasingly evident that the "different voice" which sounded "feminine" because it joins reason with emotion, the mind with the body, and the self with relationships, is in fact a human voice – in the poet Louise Gluck's terms, a wild voice, an uninitiated voice. Contrary to Snider's recollection, the little boy in Andersen's tale is not in fact silenced and shamed when he speaks in his unbridled voice. True, his father dismisses his resistance as "innocent prattle" (doing, as Snider observes, what many parents do to protect their children from the censure they fear will follow any form of resistance). But the townspeople listen and they begin to murmur: "The emperor is wearing no clothes."

We are back to Greta and Darnella, teenage girls, whose resisting voices were heard and responded to, whose protest had an outsize effect.

Here's how I understand it. From a developmental standpoint, it is an advantage that girls are of less interest than boys to a patriarchal order. If a little girl comes to school wearing pants, nobody gets ruffled, but if a boy arrives wearing a dress, a letter has to be sent out to parents. Between the ages of 4 and 7 children are learning to know the world as it is; by adolescence, children have developed the capacity to think about thinking and to differentiate how things are from how things are said to be. Listening to girls on the cusp of adolescence narrate their experiences in coming of age, my colleagues and I heard a split not between appearance and reality, but between experience and what was socially constructed as reality. Hence the pressures on girls to silence the voice of experience so as not to challenge the status quo.

Within a patriarchal order, a woman's voice becomes disruptive, precisely because she is positioned to see what cannot be seen (the vulnerability or nakedness of men) and to say what cannot be said if things are to continue in the way they have been. Think of #MeToo.

As Naomi Snider likes to say, if women's voices weren't threatening there would not be the need to silence women.

Which brings me to the betrayal of what's right. I find it striking that both Greta Thunberg and Darnella Frazier speak of what's right. "It wasn't right," Frazier says when asked to explain why she filmed George Floyd's murder. "This is all wrong," Greta Thunberg says. "I shouldn't be standing here. I should be back in school on the other side of the ocean. Yet you all come to us young people for hope. How dare you? You have stolen my dreams and my childhood with your empty words." Greta, who dares to say what adults refuse to acknowledge, frames their denial as a relational betrayal. "How dare you?" In a recent interview she explained that "the great thing about youth is that you're not blinded by realpolitik and the assumption of compromise." Her Asperger's, she says, is her superpower, because it insulates her from the voices and pressures that might otherwise lead her to forget what she knows.[19]

"Your silence will not protect you," Audre Lorde warned in the 1980s.[20]

Greta Thunberg and Darnella Frazier knew this. The clarity of their voices is inescapable, insisting we see that what is happening is not right and that we act. He was suffering, he was in pain, it is not right. If you don't care about my future, why should I?

From my studies with girls and from the later studies with boys that followed, I learned to ask new questions about development. I also learned to listen differently to adults. Where is the emotionally intelligent voice of the 4- or 5-year-old boy? What would it take to hear the honest, perceptive voice of the 10- or 11-year-old girl?

At the end of the Harvard Project, I joined with a colleague, Terrence Real, an experienced family and couples therapist, in a project designed to answer these questions. I had spent more than ten years listening to girls and women – to their voices and also their silences; I then listened to the voices of young boys and to their fathers. In that time, my ear became tuned to the difference between the actual voice of children in the times prior to their initiation into the gender codes and scripts that we are all familiar with, where men are strong and women are selfless, where men have selves and women have relationships. That is, before an emotionally open voice came to sound "babyish" to boys and an honest voice came to be heard by girls as "stupid," or "crazy."

The study with Real was small, but I will never forget the experience. In exchange for participating in our research, Terry and I saw men and women who had reached a point of impasse in their relationship with one another. Terry listened for the residues of trauma – the ways in which the past shapes the present and impedes people's ability to love and be loved. I had a different question: what if I listened for the actual voices, not the remembered voices but the actual voices of 4-year-old boys and 11-year-old girls – would these voices show a path leading out of the impasse? Was the impasse in part a residue of initiation? To my astonishment, I found that these voices of children in the years prior to initiation, unconstrained by the gender codes of patriarchy, were accessible to adults. All I needed to do was to question the culture that had driven them into silence.

Would you like to know what I think or would you like to know what I really think? Would you like to hear how I feel or would you like to hear how I actually feel? If I were to be quite honest ... Is that true? Do you really feel that way? Do you believe that?

In the end, then, my story is not about women; it's about what it means to be human. Yet girls' voices hold a key given the ability of girls to narrate both their resistance and their accommodation to an initiation that would lead them to internalize the ideologies of white supremacy and patriarchy, that would have them silence the voice that says what they really feel and think and want and know, and cover that voice with a voice that is readily mistaken for their own. The biggest surprise of my research has been the discovery of how much people know, and how accessible the under-voice is, once you question the cover.

My all-time favorite example, because it took me completely by surprise, comes from the study of couples in crisis. Phil and Sonya (I've changed their names) were leaders in their progressive church, advocates for women's rights. They had reached an impasse in their marriage because Sonya would not answer Phil's question: Was she sleeping with that guy (a colleague at her work)?

Why ask her if you know the answer?, I said, but that didn't get me very far. Instead, Phil explained, "it's the ultimate nightmare: her in the arms of another man."

It's not that I don't know the culture in which this is the ultimate nightmare and also a justification for violence. I know about the Trojan War; I know that in American society within living memory, a man who came upon his wife with a lover, *in flagrante delicto* as it's said, could kill them both with relative impunity – that is, suffering only very reduced legal consequences.

Still, I could think of worse nightmares. So it was a real question on my part, when I asked Phil: "Why is that the ultimate nightmare?"

It was his answer that blew me away. Because nothing I had read about men and masculinity or voice and relationships prepared me for what followed.

In response to my question, Phil made what psychologically speaking was a complete U-turn, saying, "The ultimate nightmare really for me" – are you hearing the word "really"? – "is never being able to show her how I really feel," – there it is again – "to be a family man and to open my heart and to love her."[21]

I learned to listen for this under-voice. I discovered how it is cued by the words "actually" and "really," and by the phrase, "to be honest." It often sounds different, at once familiar and surprising – this voice we recognize as human. To hear it, you may need to question the cover voice – the patriarchal voice, which is in fact adaptive. This means knowing the culture, its macro-ideologies and their effects on psychology; it means looking through the lens of resistance and accommodation – and remembering the tale of the emperor's new clothes.

Remember the young boy who has not yet learned to *not see* what is right in front of his eyes and who says what he sees: the emperor is naked. Then, as a spur to doing something to preserve the future, recall the voices of adolescent girls who see what is happening and say it's not right. And then think of the townspeople who murmur their agreement, because to them it has now become obvious: the emperor is naked, the earth is on fire, a man is being murdered.

2

Why Nobody Talks about the Abortion Decisions

The abortion decision study was the nub, the heart of the matter. Listening to women who, in the immediate aftermath of Roe *v.* Wade, were deciding whether to continue or to end a pregnancy, led me to hear and to pay attention to a different way of speaking about self and about morality. I discovered what questions I needed to ask in order to elicit what otherwise remained unspoken, the conversation under the conversation. The abortion decision study was the origin, the impetus for writing about a different voice and the spur to my thinking about an ethic of care. And yet it's almost never talked about – in discussions of *In a Different Voice,* in books and conferences on care ethics.

As prelude to that conversation, here are three key points.

First, the political context. In 1973, the US Supreme Court in Roe *v.* Wade affirmed as a constitutional right a woman's right to decide whether to continue or to abort a pregnancy. In essence, the highest court in the land affirmed a woman's right to have a voice in making

this decision, albeit with certain constraints and in con-
sultation with her doctor, but nevertheless a decisive
voice and a right to make the choice. In this, the authority of the court was pitted against other authorities such
as the church or fathers, so that the authorities themselves were in conflict. But by legitimizing a woman's
voice and her right to make this decision, the court also
was countering a longstanding tradition that equates
goodness in women with selflessness. This is the morality of the Angel in the House, the icon of Coventry
Patmore's nineteenth-century poem and immortalized
by Virginia Woolf – the endlessly caring woman who is
"utterly unselfish," who "never had a mind or a wish of
her own."[1]

Second, the psychological context. Kohlberg derived
his six stages of moral development from his longitu-
dinal study of seventy-two white boys, varied in social
class and followed from adolescence into adulthood.[2]
The stages were explicitly, in Kohlberg's terms, stages
of moral reasoning within a framework where, as
Socrates put it, there is only one virtue and its name is
justice. Kohlberg referred to his stages as stages of justice reasoning, and his moral stages aligned with, and
in fact were contingent on, Piaget's stages of cognitive
development, which tracked the shift from concrete to
formal operational thought. Kohlberg's stages of moral
development also ran parallel to stage theories of ego or
identity development, part of a paradigm that had been
unquestioned, where, as I note in the opening sentence
of my 1977 essay, "The arc of developmental theory
leads from infantile dependence to adult autonomy,
tracing a path characterized by an increasing differen-
tiation of self from other and a progressive freeing of

47

thought from contextual constraints" – a path marked by steps toward autonomy and rationality, seen as the hallmarks of maturity.[3] In their focus on separateness, theorists of psychological development overlooked the reality of interdependence, failing to acknowledge what to Martin Luther King was self-evident: "We are caught in an inescapable network of mutuality, tied in a single garment of destiny. What affects one directly affects all indirectly"; or, as John Donne saw centuries before climate change had made it apparent: "No man is an island, entire of itself."[4]

And third, with this political and psychological backdrop in mind, the abortion decision study and care ethics. My study is a snapshot of an historic moment. By affirming a woman's right to have a voice and to make a choice, the Supreme Court in Roe paved the way for a woman to question the internal prohibitions that may have kept her from listening to herself as well as to others, or speaking not only for others but also for herself. If the Court wasn't silencing her, why was she silencing herself?

I began Chapter 3 of In a Different Voice, "Concepts of Self and Morality," with quotations from interviews with college women, Harvard students – or Radcliffe students as they were called at the time – who had enrolled in Lawrence Kohlberg's 1971 course on moral and political choice. The most salient theme in these women's responses to questions such as, "If you had to say what morality means to you, how would you sum it up?," was a concern about hurting, a wish not to hurt others and the hope that in morality lies a way of resolving conflicts so no one will be hurt. A second note these women sounded was a sense of vulnerability that impeded them from taking a stand, what George Eliot had characterized as the girl's "susceptibility" to adverse judgments by others which stems from her lack of power and consequent inability "to do something in the world."[5]

With Roe *v.* Wade, however, the parameters shifted. Women now had the power to choose, and the abortion decision study caught the psychological ramifications of this shift. This is also one reason why, from the outset, the Court's decision became politically embattled, to the point where, now, it has been reversed.

It was clear to me from the beginning that anchoring my discussion of care ethics in the abortion decision study led me to an understanding of care and care ethics that was at odds with the morality of the Angel in the House. Because, of all the things one can imagine the Angel doing, abortion is not on the list. Instead:

> When a woman considers whether to continue or abort a pregnancy, she contemplates a decision that affects both self and other and engages directly the critical moral issue of hurting. Since the choice is ultimately hers and therefore one for which she is responsible, it raises precisely those questions of judgment that have been most problematic for women. Now she is asked whether she wishes to interrupt that stream of life which for centuries has immersed her in the passivity of dependence while at the same time imposing on her the responsibility for care. Thus, the abortion decision brings to the core of feminine apprehension, to what Joan Didion calls "the irreconcilable difference of it – that sense of living one's deepest life underwater, that dark involvement with blood and birth and death," the adult questions of responsibility and choice.[6]

The key terms here are: self and others, hurting, life and death, responsibility and choice, women and care. Because the abortion decision study was the spur that led me to think and to write about care ethics, my understanding of care was not linked to idealized images of caring or of women. Conceived in this context, care ethics engaged the critical issues of responsibility and choice in situations where hurting was inescapable and matters of life and death were at stake. To the question "Can one be a good woman and have an abortion?", I added: "Can one be a good woman and have a voice?"

The words "selfish" and "responsible" recurred throughout the interviews with women, delineating the parameters of moral choice. Defining the moral problem as one of obligation to exercise care and avoid hurt, women would use the word "selfish" to denote the infliction of hurt, considered immoral in its reflection of unconcern, while the expression of care was seen as the fulfilment of moral responsibility. It was their reiterative use of the words "selfish" and "responsible" in talking about moral conflict and choice that set these women apart from the men whom Kohlberg had studied, and pointed toward a different understanding of morality and what moral choice entails. As women moved into and then, for some, beyond the conventions of feminine goodness to question the equation of goodness with selflessness, they came to a key insight: for a woman to render herself selfless – seemingly without a voice of her own – meant to be absent rather than to be present, with herself and with others. To be careful rather than careless in deciding whether to continue or abort a pregnancy, it was imperative that she be present.

In my understanding, this was the psychological transformation precipitated by this historical moment: the political shift that gave women a legitimate voice had placed them in conflict with moral traditions that linked women's goodness to women's silence. As a side note, though one to which I will return, I think this is why abortion remains so contentious, because what is at stake in the so-called right to choose is a woman's right to have a voice, to speak for herself and thus to break a silence that is essential to maintaining a patriarchal order.

This point is illustrated by the Texas ruling that not only prohibited abortion after six weeks following a woman's last menstrual period, but also subjected anyone who came to the aid of a woman seeking an abortion after that deadline to a fine of at least $10,000. If we envision a girl who becomes pregnant after having been raped by a stranger or a member of her family, in which case it's called incest, she may not even have kept track of her last menstrual period; with the Texas law imposing a penalty on anyone who in any way assists her in ending the pregnancy, a wall of silence has in effect been erected around her.

In my interviews with pregnant women in the mid-1970s, I was struck by a woman's use of the word "selfish" to characterize whatever it was that she wanted to do – whether to have the baby or to have an abortion – whereas doing what others wanted her to do or thought she should do was "responsible" and "good." I remember Nina, a woman in her mid-twenties. Her partner, it could have been her husband, was a law student and, as she explained, she was planning to have an abortion because he depended on her support to finish law school. That is, he wanted her to abort the pregnancy. I remember saying I understood that, but what did she want to do? She looked at me as if to ask how I could even raise such a question. "What's wrong with doing something for someone you love?" she asked me. "Nothing," I said, and repeated my question.

After several iterations of this conversation, with the word "selfish" ringing in my ears, I began asking women: "If it's good to be empathic with people and responsive to people's needs and concerns, you're a person; why is it selfish to respond to yourself?" And in that historical moment, woman after woman said: "Good question."

That was the epiphany in my writing about care ethics. A political shift was precipitating or laying the ground for a psychological transformation. At the core of this transformation was an understanding of relationship and responsibility that called into question the opposition of selfishness and selflessness. Given the interdependence of self and other, it was necessary to include them both within the compass of one's care and concern, that is, to be careless with neither. Since moral dilemmas arise in situations where hurt is inescapable, there is no "right" or "good" solution. Rather than seeking justification, the moral imperative becomes "an injunction to care, a responsibility to discern and alleviate the 'real and recognizable trouble' of this world."[7]

Sharon, a woman in her thirties, when questioned about the right way to make a moral decision, articulates this shift: "The only way I know is to try to be as awake as possible, to try to know the range of what you feel, to try to consider all that's involved, to be as aware as you can of what's going on, as conscious as you can of where you're walking." Asked if there are principles that guide her, she explains:

> The principle would have something to do with responsibility, responsibility and caring about yourself and others. But it's not that on the one hand you choose to be responsible and on the other hand you choose to be irresponsible. Both ways you can be responsible. That's why there's not just a principle that once you take hold of you settle. The principle put into practice here is still going to leave you with conflict.[8]

Writing forty years later, Sandra Laugier, a moral philosopher and professor at the Sorbonne, characterizes this approach to moral problem-solving as "a paradigm of attention." She explains that "the thought of care emphasizes responsiveness to particular situations, to textures whose salient moral traits are perceived with acuity by a more perceptive and attentive stance."[9] Within the conventions of moral theory, reasoning about care can sound evasive or irrational. A stereotype of femininity. As Laugier observes, "mainstream moral philosophy is deaf to the different voice, and thus omits an entire segment of humanity."[10]

Reflecting on "What Gender Does to Moral Philosophy," Laugier doesn't shy away from the word "women." To her, the different voice, "explicitly and for the first time, marks the need to bring women's *voices* into ordinary human conversation." By this she means conversations about ordinary things in Wittgenstein's sense, "remarks on the natural history of human beings . . . observations which no one has doubted, but which have escaped remark only because they are always before our eyes."[11]

Laugier does not refer to the abortion decision study – it is 11-year-old Amy who exemplifies for her the difference in the different voice. Yet what Laugier puts forward in her exposition of "Amy's ethics" is a philosophical explication of what Sharon and other women who took part in the abortion decision study say in explaining their thinking about the choice they are making. In her chapter for the 2022 book *Thinking with Women Philosophers*, Laugier cites as the lasting contribution of the different voice "not only its promotion of an ethics of attention, but a starting point for an *epistemology* of ethics: the revelation that moral philosophy – the heart of the discipline – is not only historically the work of men, but is, in its very concepts, a patriarchal form of thought."[12]

To Laugier, the different voice is in itself indelibly political because

> the very definition of ethics in philosophy is achieved *by means of* the exclusion of an entire domain and a group of people [usually women and often women of color] whose contribution is essential to life and to the survival of society, and by the massive denial of the work done to guarantee the functioning of the world.

Perspectives of care, she writes,

> contain a fundamental claim about the importance of care for human life, and about the importance of importance itself; the importance of an unacknowledged dimension of morality. Thus, the ethic of care constitutes a radical challenge to dominant moral philosophy.[13]

Care work, for the most part underpaid and undervalued, has been burdened by the gendering of caring as "feminine," by its association with women and those who, like women (however idealized), are considered lesser, notably people of color. In reality, they do the lion's share of care work, including for people who claim to be independent and thus not to need care. Hence the people who care for them must be invisible, and do their work in silence. Yet by insisting on speaking about women at a time when the term itself has become suspect, Laugier reminds us,

> It is because the work and activities of care have traditionally fallen to women that care is first and foremost a women's issue. Considering the social, moral, and political importance of care obliges us to refer to "women," one of the categories to whom the work of care has principally been assigned, and to ask "What is the nature of a democratic conversation that excludes that which makes it materially possible?"[14]

The abortion decision study called for a radical shift in the framework of moral theory. The different voice changes the voice of the conversation. It challenges what had been taken as fundamental or foundational – the opposition of egoism and altruism, selfishness and selflessness – on grounds of ignoring fragility and vulnerability and overlooking the reality of interdependence. The abortion decision study called upon us neither to idealize nor to denigrate women, but rather to listen to women's voices and to see the obvious. Care work, largely done by women and often women of color, is essential to human life.

It was easier simply not to talk about it.

3

Enter Eve

I teach a class on listening and, for many years now, I begin with Freud – the case of Elisabeth von R. from *Studies on Hysteria*.[1] Freud's account of his initial foray into psychoanalysis has become something of a *Baedeker* for my students, a guide they can follow as they embark on a journey of psychological inquiry. Freud's precision in laying out his own path to discovery serves as a model for how to proceed in doing research because he records the steps that he took (and also his missteps) in coming to understand what at first were mysteries: why Elisabeth suffers great pains in walking and, in her own words, could not "take a single step forward,"[2] why, as he observes along the way, a "group of ideas relating to her love had already become separated from her knowledge,"[3] and, lastly, why, when Elisabeth claims not to know what is happening to her, does she in fact know, although, as Freud notes in the case of Miss Lucy R., she may not know that she knows it.[4] Since we can both know and not know what we know, since psychic pain can be converted into physical pain and find symbolic modes of expression, Freud concluded that a special method was necessary for psychological inquiry. To discover the cause of his patients' suffering, he had to gain access to what his patients knew – aspects of their experience that they had dissociated from themselves and that remained outside their awareness. Thus, he invented psychoanalysis, with its method of free association. If he could connect Elisabeth's love with her knowledge, he might be able to help her move forward.

In addition to reading Freud's case history at the start of the term, we read Piaget's introduction to *The Child's Conception of the World* – a brilliant essay on method where Piaget pinpoints the limitations of both testing and observation, bound as they are to the tester or observer's conception of the world. Only by using a clinical method, Piaget explains, can one discover not where someone fits on your map of the world but how another person conceives reality.[5]

And finally, we read Audre Lorde, for her reminder that "the master's tools will never dismantle the master's house."[6]

In their early forays into psychological inquiry, Freud and Piaget saw the need to forge new methods: free association and the clinical interrogatory or *méthode clinique*. These were tools that could dismantle the master's house, in part by revealing what women know, including about the master, and also by exposing the master's house for what it is: a construction of reality rather than a repository of truth. Yet once Freud and Piaget discovered how radical these methods are, they pulled back, settling back, it is tempting to say, into the master's house and becoming, in effect, the master.

In many years of teaching my class on listening, first at Harvard and now at NYU, I have witnessed the power of association to undo dissociation. Listening for voices that had been silenced or that speak at the margins, picking up on the conversation under the conversation and noticing when the framework shifts, I have come to question whether what may pass for objective methods include ways of holding the master's house in place. In the process, I have come to suspect that psychoanalysis and to some extent psychology more generally have been contested, not to say embattled, in part because in fact they offer us tools that can dismantle the master's house. Yet to the extent that we continue to live in that house, we are, to say the least, conflicted.

It was by accident, so to speak, through a process of association that the biblical Eve came into my thinking about psychology and morality and relationships between women and men. I am writing a novel about a dancer, and, as sometimes happens in writing fiction, characters arrive with their names. My dancer came with her name, Eve, and although at first I didn't think much about it, later I wondered: Eve? Why Eve? And this in turn led me to reread the Garden of Eden story.

I thought I knew the story, but there on the page, right in front of me, was something I had overlooked: an act on the part of the first woman that changed my way of seeing her. It disrupted what I had thought of as the story. Then in the spring of 2017, I was told something about the creation of woman that struck me as totally improbable. And yet profoundly true. This was a disruption at a much deeper level.

I'll start with the story. Adam and Eve are in the Garden of Eden. Actually, she's called "the woman" until they are about to leave the garden, when Adam names her *Chava*, or Eve, from the Hebrew word *chaya*, meaning life. Because, the Bible explains, she is the one who will bring forth life. She will be the mother.

But that's not where it starts. The story begins with the serpent, the "most cunning of all the beasts in the field," who asks the woman, "Can you eat from all the trees in this garden?" and she says, "Yes, all but the one in the center and if we eat from that tree or touch the fruit, we will die." No, the serpent tells her, you will not die. Your eyes will be opened and you will be as gods, knowing good and evil.

We know this as a story about forbidden knowledge, about temptation and transgression, about man and woman, about mortality. What I hadn't known, what I literally hadn't seen or taken in, is what follows the interchange between the woman and the serpent. The woman now has been told two conflicting things: you will die, you will not die. So what does she do?

She looks at the tree.

The woman is not the dupe of the serpent, or seduced by the prospect of being as gods. In the face of conflicting authorities and truths, she decides to see for herself and – she acts on her own perceptions. Here's the King James Version: "And when the woman *saw* that the tree was good for food, and that it was pleasant to the eyes, and a tree to be desired to make one wise, she took of the fruit thereof, and did eat, and gave also unto her husband with her; and he did eat" (the italics are mine).[7] In Robert Alter's 2018 translation "And the woman *saw* that the tree was good for eating and that it was lust to the eyes and the tree was lovely to look at, and she took of its fruit and ate, and she also gave to her man with her, and he ate" (again, the italics are mine).[8]

Essentially the same. This could be the story of any woman or everywoman or for that matter anyone who, seeing a fruit that is good for food and pleasing to the eye and a source of nourishment or wisdom (like fish if you consider fish brain food), takes it and eats it, and, when nothing happens (no one dies, no one feels ashamed or moves to cover their nakedness), gives some to the person who is with them. An ordinary story.

But once Adam has eaten the fruit, that's when the story shifts. Suddenly Adam and the woman are hiding from God and using fig leaves to cover their nakedness. When, in the cool of the evening, God comes into the garden, he calls not for the woman but for Adam. And then the blaming starts. Adam blames the woman, the woman blames the serpent. God punishes them for their transgression. To the woman he says, "And for your man shall be your longing, and he shall rule over you." To Adam; he says, "Because you listened to the voice of your wife" and disobeyed my commandments, "cursed be the soil for your sake, with pangs shall you eat from it all the days of your life." Or, in the more familiar King James translation, "in sorrow shalt thou eat of it all the days of your life."[9]

That story also we know. The story of it was all her fault.

But here's what truly astonished me. In 2017, I was invited to speak at the Knesset, the Israeli Parliament, by women members from the center and center-left parties. The session was held in a conference room of the Knesset building in Jerusalem, and about 150 people, mostly women, were invited to attend. In the question period following my talk, one of the women, an international human rights lawyer, asked me: "Have you heard of *ezer k'negdo*?"

No. I had no idea what she was talking about.

She translated the Hebrew words: *ezer* means helper, though not in the sense of a servant or a subordinate because God is an *ezer*, someone who has the power to help. And *k'negdo* means by opposing him. "Confronting" is another translation according to my friend, the Israeli philosopher Moshe Halbertal. It means to be opposite someone, to face them, or, as the woman lawyer said that day in Jerusalem, to pull them in an opposite direction.

Ezer k'negdo is from the book of Genesis, from the second creation story, where God creates Adam, the earthling, the human, because God needed someone to till the soil. Seeing that Adam is lonely, God creates the animals to keep him company. But then God sees that this is not sufficient. What Adam needs, God sees, is an *ezer k'negdo*, someone who will help him by opposing him. And so God creates woman.

I was stunned. How come we don't know this? Or maybe you do. How come I didn't know this?

And in one sense the answer is clear. *Negdo* is not translated. It is simply left out. "Help meet" is the King James translation. "Helpmate" is an alternative; no whiff of opposition. The New English Bible says "partner." Robert Alter translates *ezer k'negdo* as "sustainer beside him," adding in a footnote that the Hebrew phrase *ezer k'negdo* "is notoriously difficult to translate," although why this is so remains a mystery.[10] A law student in my seminar on resisting injustice, a Hebrew speaker from

Australia, had no trouble translating the words. To him, the meaning was obvious.

In his footnote, Alter writes that *negdo* "means 'alongside him,' 'opposite him,' 'a counterpart to him'." It's the notion of opposition that gets lost. As if it were inconceivable that the words could mean what on the face of it they mean. Or more to the point, impossible to think that man, the human, needed a woman to help him by opposing him – or confronting him, or challenging him, or questioning him, or facing him, or pulling him in a direction opposite to the one where, left to himself, he most likely would go. And whatever god said this – whoever wrote the words *ezer k'negdo* into the story of woman's creation – that voice could not be listened to, in contrast to the familiar story about seduction and disobedience. Because truly, what man or what God could even conceive that a man, a human, would need a woman to help him in this way?

There is nothing difficult about the words themselves. *Ezer* or, for that matter, *negdo*, an ordinary word *neged*. In everyday Hebrew it means "against," and with the "o," "against him or it," like a team in basketball playing against another team. It's the concept of a woman's opposition being helpful to man that is "notoriously difficult" to stomach.

Yet somebody, some ancient sage, left tracks, footprints in the sand. To follow these tracks then leads to a very different reading of the Adam and Eve story and also, I would say, to theories of self and morality and development. Because in this reading, the woman, an afterthought in this conception of the world, sees where things are heading when knowledge of good and evil belongs solely to a Lord God on high and man is barred from grasping what is in nature (as a tree is in nature), including in his own nature. In short, somewhere, someone long ago saw that, under these conditions, the human would need someone to pull him in an opposite direction, away from the path that will lead to the woman becoming subjugated to him, out of the story that ends with "And he shall rule over her." Where he is the human and she is the mother. In short, the patriarchal story.

I am riveted by these traces of an alternative story, set down long ago and eclipsed by what we have come to know as "the story." Why, we may wonder, does this insight into a man's need have to be covered? When I came upon a passage in one of Toni Morrison's novels explaining why, I realized that, at least to some women, this is no secret. The passage in question is from *Beloved*. It is about Paul D.'s relationship to Sethe, the mother of Beloved. Like Sethe, Paul D. had been a slave on the Garner plantation. Speaking in Paul D.'s voice, Morrison writes, "Sethe, she's fixed me and I can't break it." The passage continues:

> What? A grown man fixed by a girl . . . and fucking her or not was not the point, it was not being able to stay [in her house] or go where he wishes . . . the danger was in losing Sethe because he was not man enough to break out, so he needed her, Sethe, to help him, to know about it, and it shamed him to have to ask the woman he wanted to protect to help him do it. God damn it to hell.[11]

The danger was in losing Sethe because . . . he needed her . . . to help him. But, as Morrison had written just a few lines earlier, "he was a man and a man could do what he would." Therefore, his needing Sethe to know about it and to help him break out or to fix it shamed him. It made him not a man.[12]

So here we are.

This is the story we need to disrupt, and we need to do so before it's too late. If we ask what Paul D. needed Sethe to help him break out of and what he needed her to fix, Morrison's novel answers the question. Paul D. needed Sethe to help him break out of the emotional lockdown that besets a man in patriarchy: namely, the conception of manhood that, in Morrison's haunting image, forces Paul D. to carry his tears locked up inside him, in "that tobacco tin buried in his chest where a red heart used to be. Its lid rusted shut."[13] For Paul D. to break out means to break that tin open; to "fix it" means to experience the shame he would feel in releasing emotions that would cause him to believe "I am not a man," which, in fact, is what he wants to tell Sethe but cannot bring himself to say.[14]

Let me be very clear about what I am and am not saying. In the book of Genesis, there are two creation stories. In the one told at the very outset, in Genesis 1, God creates the world in six days, starting with heaven and earth and ending with humans, "male and female created he them." No hierarchy, no either/or binary, just humans, male and female. It could be a spectrum. In the second creation story, Genesis 2, on the day the Lord God – for he is now called Lord God, both in the King James Version and by Alter – on the day the Lord God made the earth and the heavens, he fashioned the human from the soil (*humus*, or in Hebrew, *adama*), and blew into his nostrils the breath of life so there would be someone to till the soil. In contrast to Genesis 1, this creation story is a patriarchal story. In the beginning, the Lord God creates Adam, the earthling, who is man; initially there is no thought of woman. But then God sees that Adam is lonely – you know how it goes – and this in turn leads to the recognition that what Adam needs is an *ezer k'negdo*, so God puts Adam to sleep and out of his side creates an *ezer k'negdo* for him. That is, he creates woman.

What I'm saying is that, embedded within this second, patriarchal creation story is a story of resistance to patriarchy, along with the insight that Adam will need to resist patriarchy (and like Paul D. will need someone to help him do it). So there are in effect three creation stories: the first creation story in Genesis 1 ("male and female created he them"); the second creation story in Genesis 2, where God creates Adam, man, and what follows is directed by man's needs – that is, the patriarchal story. And then, within the patriarchal story is a resistance story, where God creates woman to help Adam resist patriarchy.

It's not that she's right and he's wrong. Rather it is, as Toni Morrison sees, that he needs her to help him do what he cannot do on his own because he is a man. That is, he needs someone who is not a man to oppose what, as a man, he cannot break out of or fix without calling his virility into question: the lockdown of his heart.

There are many ways to read the story of woman made from Adam's rib, but in my reading the words *ezer k'negdo* are the tip-off. What strikes me is that some wise person way back then saw that within this patriarchal conception of the world, Adam, the man, will be vulnerable in a way that will lead him to need a helper who is strong (an *ezer*) and who, seeing where this is heading – into hiding and covering, blaming and shaming, punishment and suffering, entrapment and domination – will help him by pulling him in an opposite direction. Someone, a woman, a being, a human who is not foreign to him, but who is created out of a side of himself. Someone in touch with his humanity.

In the layered creation story in the book of Genesis, the patriarchal story is an overlay. It displaces an earlier story about humans and contains within itself the seeds of its undoing. The agent of this disruption is a woman, and in this light it makes sense that the "different voice" was heard as a woman's voice or a "feminine" voice. In truth, it is a feminist voice, because the story it disrupts is a patriarchal story. With the disruption now spreading through the human sciences in the form of a paradigm shift or relational turn, relational capacities such as empathy and emotional intelligence, once considered "feminine," are recognized for what they are: human strengths.

Now the different voice can be heard for what it is: a human voice. Our voice, in the beginning. A voice that joins thinking and feeling, self and relationship, mind and body. And with this realization comes the recognition that separations once hailed as milestones of progress (the separation of reason from emotion, mind from body, self from relationships) are, in fact, manifestations of injury or trauma.

Thus, when we encounter someone who is lacking in empathy or who appears relationally clueless, or seemingly has no voice, we are prompted to ask, "What happened?" What happened to this human being?

Studies with children and adolescents in the 1980s and '90s speak to this question. They illuminate a process of initiation that requires dissociation. The phrases

"I don't know" and "I don't care" marked this rite of passage in children's lives. An injunction – "don't" – came between "I" and knowing or caring, so that in becoming young women, girls would not know what they knew on the basis of their own experience and, in becoming men, boys would not care about what in truth they cared about deeply.

But what if this dissociation does not happen?

Greta Thunberg was 8 when she first learned about climate change. *Time* magazine reports that her primary school teacher had shown "a video of its effects: starving polar bears, extreme weather and flooding. The teacher explained that it was all happening because of climate change. Afterward the entire class felt glum, but the other kids were able to move on. Thunberg couldn't. She began to feel extremely alone."[15]

I have asked myself why. Why is it that a young girl managed to galvanize the realization that first struck her when she was 8 and to mobilize people on a scale that climate change activists had not previously managed, despite their greater knowledge and resources and, to be sure, social skills? As she is quick to acknowledge, Greta is on the spectrum; she has been diagnosed with Asperger's syndrome, along with obsessive compulsive disorder and selective mutism. Which is why, she explains, in her TED talk, "I speak only when I feel it is necessary."[16]

When Greta was 11 she fell into a deep depression. As the *Time* reporters write:

> For months she stopped speaking almost entirely, and ate so little that she was nearly hospitalized; that period of malnutrition would later stunt her growth. Her parents took

time off from work to nurse her through what her father remembers as a period of "endless sadness," and Thunberg herself recalls feeling confused. "I couldn't understand how that could exist, that existential threat, and yet we didn't prioritize it," she says. "I was maybe in a bit of denial, like, 'That can't be happening, because if that were happening, then the politicians would be taking care of it'."[17]

At first her father had tried to reassure her that everything would be okay. But, "as he read more about the climate crisis, he found his own words rang hollow. 'I realized that she was right and I was wrong'."[18]

Like the child in "The Tale of the Emperor's New Clothes" (in Andersen's fairytale it's a young boy) who says what in one sense is obvious – the emperor is naked – Greta was speaking the truth: the planet is on fire.

Time reports:

> In an effort to comfort their daughter, the family began changing their habits to reduce their emissions. They mostly stopped eating meat, installed solar panels, began growing their own vegetables and eventually gave up flying – a sacrifice for Thunberg's mother, [an opera singer] who performs throughout Europe.[19]

"We did all these things," her father explains, "basically not really to save the climate, we didn't care much about that initially . . . We did it to make her happy and to get her back to life." Slowly Greta began to eat and talk again. As her father said, after she began striking, she indeed "came back to life."[20]

To the annual gathering of CEOs and world leaders at Davos, Switzerland, Greta said, "I want you to feel the fear I feel every day. And then I want you to act."[21]

To the members of the US Congress who thanked her when she visited the Capitol, she said virtually the same thing: "Do something."

Greta's Asperger's may have insulated her from an initiation that in the name of goodness or for the sake of inclusion would have kept her from saying in this unadorned voice what is so patently, nakedly true. And my intention is not to romanticize Asperger's syndrome, but rather to ask: Why has this voice found such resonance?

My answer is simple: because it is a voice we recognize, a human voice. At once familiar and surprising. A voice we know and then learned to dismiss as naive or unpleasant. A voice that puts us on edge, in part because it leads us to question losses we may have justified as necessary and to revisit sacrifices we may have made in the name of manhood or honor or becoming a good woman, or for the sake of having relationships and keeping the peace and making our way in the world. In a world where, to be a man, a man must blind himself to his vulnerability and a woman must act as though she is selfless and has no voice of her own, the human voice is a voice of resistance.

Teaching at a university, I am surprised when even now I hear a woman dismiss her own experience as "subjective," or deem it "selfish" to ask what is her question, what *she* really wants to know. Recently I watched a student waver when her faculty advisor told her that to draw on her own experience in framing the question for her thesis (which was about women) would be "too anecdotal" and "not scientific." He warned her that no one would take her or her work seriously. As someone invested in the seriousness of her work, I saw the need to disrupt this story.

In the seminar on resisting injustice in the Fall of 2019, Gary Uter, a top student, titled his final paper: "BoysIIMen." Among his insights into the transition to manhood, the one I found most original was his perception that patriarchy "is in and of itself a form of double consciousness." Uter, an African American law student, was headed for one of New York's most prestigious firms. He was inspired by W. E. B. DuBois's *The Souls of Black Folk*, where DuBois describes double consciousness:

> It is a peculiar sensation, this double consciousness, this sense of always looking at one's self through the eyes of others, of measuring one's soul by the tape of a world that looks on in amused contempt and pity. One ever feels his two-ness – an American, a Negro; two souls, two thoughts, two unreconciled strivings; two warring ideals in one dark body, whose dogged strength alone keeps it from being torn asunder.[22]

Uter's insight was that this is also the struggle of men in patriarchy – the two-ness, the "peculiar sensation" of being both a man and a human; "two souls, two thoughts, two unreconciled strivings." But, Uter writes, "unlike most instances of double consciousness, the patriarchal double consciousness is one where the owner of this consciousness is expected to deny its existence. Under patriarchy, a man cannot acknowledge that patriarchy is a social construct."[23]

It is this double consciousness that Greta Thunberg lacks; chalk it up to the Asperger's. She is single-minded. Yet it is hard to contest it when she says, tongue in cheek because she has a sense of irony, if we don't care about her future, why should she? I hear her voice as a primal voice, a human voice, a pre-initiated voice. It sounds familiar because we were once there, seeing the world in black and white, which is how Greta characterizes her way of seeing, before we learned that things are more complicated, that there is more than one way of looking at a problem, and yes, the planet is in peril but we also have to go to school.

Because what was initially heard as a "different voice" is in fact a human voice, it is a voice we harbor within ourselves. Because this human voice differs from a patriarchal voice, within ourselves we contain the seeds of transformation – a way out of a highly gendered order of living held in place by men's blindness and women's silence. But it is also necessary not to minimize the disruption.

Greta Thunberg is by no means the only one saying that the rules have to be changed. The primatologist Frans de Waal has called for "a complete reassessment of our assumptions about human nature."[24]

The difficult part of *ezer k'negdo* is that it has to do with women and, more specifically, with relationships between women and men. I have yet to meet a woman in a long marriage to a man who didn't know instantly what *ezer k'negdo* is about. But they also knew not to talk about it. And the reason is obvious. In Toni Morrison's novel, Paul D. names it; Gary Uter, the star student in the resisting injustice seminar explains it. I understand, or at least I think I understand, why *ezer k'negdo* is "notoriously difficult to translate." We cannot know what it says, not because it isn't true but because it would shame a man for us to know this.

Greta says we're running out of time. This is a conundrum we need to solve. How can we do what as humans we now must do before it's too late? How can we fix it without tripping the wire that would blow things up? Because when manhood is shamed, violence is imminent.[25]

In her essay "Splitting the World Open: Connection and Disconnection among Women Teaching Girls," the educator Judith Dorney reflects that a "central part of the work of connection is in dealing with the crises that emerge as we move forward." She adds that along with whatever internal conflicts and interpersonal tensions may stand in the way of connection, there are also institutional barriers, forces that "will generally work to maintain the status quo." Traditional schooling, in her experience, "is not currently designed to hold these kinds of intense connections or to challenge the traditions and conventional power relationships."[26]

Dorney was writing about the transformative power of the Harvard Project's Women Teaching Girls/Girls Teaching Women retreats, which she had taken the lead in developing. And yet, despite the power of the retreats, the transformation was cut short, in part for the reasons she mentions. Dorney concludes, "If we all had been more aware of these [institutional] patterns and forces, I believe this could have been not just a good story but a revolutionary one."[27]

To me, that's the implication of the footprints left in the sand – what turned into, one might say, *the* patriarchal story, the story of Adam and Eve, could have taken a very different turn. Because in the end Audre Lorde is right: the master's tools will never dismantle the master's house. But there are other tools, and what's more, we have them.

4

Moral Injury

1. Betrayal of What's Right

A veteran, a member of a Long Range Reconnaissance patrol that killed innocent civilians – "a lot of fishermen and kids" – as the result of an intelligence error, says:

> What got us thoroughly fucking confused is, at that time you turn to the team and you say to the team, "Don't worry about it. Everything's fucking fine." Because that's what you're getting from upstairs.
>
> The fucking colonel says, "Don't worry about it. We'll take care of it." Y'know, uh. "We got body count!" "We have body count!" So it starts working on your head.
>
> So you know in your heart it's wrong, but at the time, here's your superiors telling you that it's okay. So, I mean, that's *okay* then, right? This is part of war. Y'know? Gung-HO! Y'know?[1]

Just listen!" Jonathan Shay tells us: "Before analyzing, before classifying, before thinking, before trying to *do* anything, we should *listen*."[2] Working with combat veterans who were suffering from severe and chronic post-traumatic stress disorders, Shay cautions us: take in the story before trying to make sense of it. Because in fact these stories don't make sense; they are stories about becoming "confused," where the confusion starts "working on your head," because "you know in your heart it's wrong" but "here's your superiors telling you that it's okay." And it's not just okay. It's "part of war" and rewarded with medals of honor. In the words of one veteran, these stories are "sacred stuff."

Yet, Shay notes, "all too often our mode of listening deteriorates into intellectual sorting with the professional grabbing the veterans' words from the air and sticking them into mental bins." We assume we know what we're hearing, that we don't really have to listen, that we've heard it all before. In this, we "resemble museum-goers whose whole experience consists of mentally saying, 'That's cubist! . . . That's El Greco!' and who never *see* anything they've looked at." As Shay reflects, "listening in this way *destroys* trust."[3]

Shay's world and mine are far apart. Shay was listening to Vietnam combat veterans, I to children in school and afterschool settings. Children and their teachers, children and their parents. Yet hearing Shay speak about moral injury, I came to a sudden, startling realization: I too had witnessed a betrayal of what's right, in a situation where the stakes were high, and where the betrayal was sanctioned by those in positions of legitimate authority. Not in the extremity of combat trauma but as part of a process of initiation that was happening in the everyday. The betrayal of what's right was a betrayal of relationship.

Speaking about the need for a way of listening that creates trust, Shay was describing my research. He had named what others had considered a disorder (a post-traumatic stress disorder) as an injury – a *moral* injury: a shattering of trust had followed a betrayal of "what's right." Something had happened that wasn't right, and yet it had been culturally sanctioned, creating a rift in the social fabric. "Healing from trauma depends on communalization of the trauma," Shay writes.[4] Because the community was complicit in the betrayal, the community has to be involved in the healing. Otherwise trust cannot be restored.

Adolescence is a crossroads in girls' lives, a place where girlhood and womanhood intersect. In *Meeting at the Crossroads*, Lyn Mikel Brown and I report a five-year study with close to 100 girls that spanned this intersection. According to standard measures of psychological development and educational progress, the girls in our study – ranging in age from 7 to 18, diverse in race, ethnicity, and social class, and educationally advantaged – were doing very well.

> Our study provides clear evidence that as these girls grow older they become less dependent on external authorities, less egocentric, or locked in their own experience or point of view, more differentiated from others in the sense of being able to distinguish their feelings and thoughts from those of other people, more autonomous in the sense of being able to rely on or take responsibility for themselves, more appreciative of the complex interplay of voices and perspectives in any relationship, more aware of the diversity of human experience and the differences between societal and cultural groups.

Yet, this clear evidence of developmental progress goes hand in hand with "a loss of voice, a struggle to authorize or take seriously their own experience – to listen to their own voices in conversation and respond to their feelings and thoughts – increased confusion, sometimes defensiveness, as well as evidence for the replacement of real with unauthentic or idealized relationships."[5]

We were picking up signs of moral injury: a betrayal of relationship had led to confusion, including confusion about relationships (the difference between real versus idealized or inauthentic connections); some girls registered the betrayal as a betrayal of what's right, some resisted the betrayal. Something didn't make sense. As the veteran said, you know in your heart it's wrong, but here's your superiors telling you that it's okay, part of war. The betrayal of relationship was also said to be okay, part of growing up.

And then it became clear that it wasn't just girls. Signs of moral injury are evident among boys, both at an earlier crossroads in their lives, roughly between 4 and 7, the time when they enter formal schooling and are called upon to establish themselves as boys, and also during the later years of high school when they know more about how to be a man. Again, relationships are on the line, along with issues of identity and inclusion. I am speaking about the work of Judy Chu and Niobe Way, about Chu's book *When Boys Become Boys: Development, Relationships, and Masculinity*, and Way's book *Deep Secrets: Boys' Friendships and the Crisis of Connection*. Relationships are in both subtitles.

"What's right" is Shay's equivalent of the Greek word *themis*. As Shay reflects:

No single English word takes in the whole sweep of a culture's definition of right and wrong; we use terms such as moral order, convention, normative expectations, ethics, and commonly understood social values. The ancient Greek word that Homer used, *themis,* encompasses all these meanings.

Yet speaking of *themis,* Shay observes that although deep assumptions of "what's right" may be culturally specific, the response to their violation is remarkably consistent: "The specific content of the Homeric warriors' *themis* was often quite different from that of American soldiers in Vietnam, but what has not changed in three millennia are violent rage and social withdrawal when deep assumptions of 'what's right' are violated."[6]

The same response across three millennia. For both Homeric warriors and Vietnam war veterans, the betrayal of what's right elicited violent rage and social withdrawal. Men who had fought in Vietnam were going berserk, going crazy, like Achilles in Homer's *Iliad*. Because something had happened that did not make sense.

At 13, Judy describes her experience of an initiation that carries with it the risk of forgetting her mind. Your mind, she says, pointing to her gut, "is sort of associated with your heart and your soul and your internal feeling and your real feelings." How can she stay in touch with what she knows in her gut and at the same time take in what she needs to take in, what is considered by her superiors, her teachers, to be knowledge? Judy arrives at a creative solution. She will separate her mind – the mind she associates with her heart and her soul and her real feelings – from her brain, which she associates with her intelligence, her smartness, and her education. Speaking of her brain, she says,

> [people] can control what they're teaching you and say, "This is right and this is wrong," that's control like into your brain. But the feeling is just with you; [the feeling] can't be changed by someone else who wants it to be this way. It can't be changed by saying, "No, this is wrong, this is right, this is wrong."[7]

There is a limit to socialization. People can tell you what is right and what is wrong but "the feeling is just with you." To Judy at 13, feeling and knowing are two different things, yet this distinction breaks down as she contrasts two kinds of knowing, "a deeper sort of knowing" that is connected with feelings, and intelligence knowing that

> sort of comes from the brain, like your intelligence part. Like your smartness, your brightness, your education part, and your feeling is something that it doesn't matter if you have an education or not, it's just like something that you can't put into words. That you can't really explain, but it's not, I don't know, it's just like a deeper sort of knowing than intelligence knowing. Because intelligence tells you "no," "bad," "yes," "good," and all that.

Speaking of the knowing that is connected with feeling, Judy explains: "Whenever I feel something bad is going to happen or feel scared or something awful, I can feel it in my stomach, a gut feeling that you are not doing something right or you are doing something that you don't really care about . . . whether it's right or wrong." This feeling, she continues, "is an internal sort of knowing, like it just has to do with like not your brain but more your mind."[8]

Yet in the course of growing up, Judy reflects, people lose their minds; "it's sort of like something that happens gradually," but "after a while, you just sort of forget your mind, because everything is being shoved at you into your brain."[9]

The worlds – Shay's world and my world – are not so far apart.

I am struck by the similar split in both contexts – a disparity between what you know in your heart, the internal sort of knowing that is just with you, and what people are telling you, including about right and wrong. The veteran says you know in your heart it's wrong but here's your superiors telling you that it's okay. Judy speaks of people "telling you ... 'This is right and this is wrong'," controlling you by controlling your brain. Controlling you by telling you how to think about morality. But as she observes, "the feeling is just with you ... the feeling can't be changed by someone else who wants it to be this way."

2. A triptych of initiation

The word "betrayal" appears repeatedly in Niobe Way's book *Deep Secrets*, used by the adolescent boys in her studies to explain why they no longer have a best friend, why they don't tell their secrets to anyone anymore. Justin describes it as something that "just happens," he doesn't know if it's "natural or whatever." But the shattering of trust is unmistakable. As Joseph says, "You can't trust nobody these days."[10]

Justin was among the majority of the boys in Way's studies – boys from a range of cultural backgrounds (Latino, Puerto Rican, Dominican, Chinese, African American, Anglo, Muslim, Russian, and so on) – who "spoke of having and wanting intimate male friendships and then gradually losing these relationships and their trust in their male peers." As a freshman and sophomore in high school, Mohammed speaks of telling his best friend all his secrets; when interviewed as a junior, he says, "I don't know. Recently ... you know I kind of changed something. Not that much, but you know I feel like there's no need to – I could keep [my feelings] to myself. You know, I'm mature enough."[11]

Fernando also talks about maturing. Asked what he sees as an ideal friendship, he begins, "You gotta be funny, truthful. I just got to have fun with you, you know." But then he says, more haltingly and with a question, "Um, you gotta, I guess, just be there for me? I guess. I don't want to sound too sissy like ... I think I've matured in certain ways ... I know how to be more of a man."[12]

Way found that in the early years of high school, boys resist the binary construction of gender that makes it "sissy-like" for them to depend on someone and want them to "just be there for me." But by the end of high school, the binary is enforced. Emotional intimacy and vulnerability have taken on a gender (girly) and a sexuality (gay). Being a man means being emotionally stoic and independent.

What at first felt unimpeded to these boys – the "trust, respect, and love" that 15-year-old Justin saw as "so deep, it's within you ... it's human nature" – had become fraught.[13] Justin doesn't know if the distance from his friends he now feels is "natural or whatever"; what he knows is, "it just happens."

The boys in Way's studies know the value of close friendships. George says that without a best friend to tell your secrets to, you would "go whacko." Chen says that without a close friend, "you go crazy." Others describe how anger builds up inside them when they don't have a best friend to talk to. Some speak of sadness, loneliness, and depression. Yet in spite of this awareness, they minimize the loss and downplay its consequences, chalking it up to maturing, to knowing "how to be more of a man."

It was the studies with girls – the ten-year Harvard Project, years that I spent listening to girls, interviewing them year after year in schools, meeting with them in weekly or week-long afterschool writing and theater clubs, going on outings with them to nature sanctuaries, museums, and historic sites like Old Sturbridge Village, and going on retreats with their women teachers – that illuminated the mechanism of betrayal. Listening to girls narrate their experiences in coming of age, my research team and I heard them describe the pressures they felt to divide their head from their heart (think of Judy), their minds from their bodies, and, most strikingly, their honest voices from their relationships. They were learning not to say what they were "really" thinking or how they "actually" felt – to keep to themselves or not trust what they knew first hand on the basis of their own experience. They were learning that if they were "to be honest" about what they were thinking and feeling, no one would want to be with them. The price of having relationships was an inner silence.

The internalization of the gender binary and hierarchy marks the psyche's induction into patriarchy. As a rule of thumb, when you hear a gender binary (human capabilities spoken of as either "masculine" or "feminine") and a hierarchy where the masculine is elevated over the feminine, (e.g., reason over emotion, self over relationships), you know you're in patriarchy, however it may be called. Organized around gender and privileging the voice of a father or fathers (*patres*), patriarchy is at odds with democracy, which rests on a premise of equal voice or equality. But patriarchy is also unnatural – at odds with our human nature. Love and empathy threaten its hierarchy of privilege and power, and our capacity to give voice to our experience breaks its silences. To maintain orders of living where some humans are considered more human than others, it is necessary that those at the top not register the feelings of those who are beneath them and for the voices of those at the bottom not to be listened to or taken seriously. But the injury goes deeper than this. To conceive of human capacities as being either "masculine" or "feminine," to divide reason from emotion and the self from relationships, is to sever connections that are essential to registering our experience and thus to navigating the human social world. As neuroscientists and experts on trauma concur, separations once viewed as signposts of development are now recognized to be manifestations of injury or trauma. The separation of reason from emotion and of the self from relationship are manifestations of moral injury.

To put it simply, the induction of the psyche into the gendered splits and divisions that undergird a patriarchal order of living forces a betrayal of what's right. The initiation into patriarchy shatters trust by making it impossible to live with integrity in relationship with others. Moral development then depends on resistance. As a healthy body resists infection, a healthy psyche resists moral injury.

The studies with girls that began in the 1980s both illuminated the resistance and highlighted what is at stake. One has only to listen to girls before the initiation sets in to hear a reading of the human social world that can be startling in its nakedness. At the beginning of Charlotte Brontë's novel, 10-year-old Jane Eyre tells her Aunt Reed, who had called her deceitful,

> I am not deceitful: if I were, I should say I loved *you*; but I declare I do not love you: I dislike you the worst of anybody in the world except John Reed, and this book about the liar, you may give to your girl, Georgiana, for it is she who tells lies, and not I . . . People think you a good woman, but you are bad, hard-hearted . . . I'll let everybody at Lowood know what you are, and what you have done.[14]

We know this voice. It has been heard and recorded over and over again. Through vast stretches of time and across a great diversity of cultures, the voice is unmistakable. It's the voice of Iphigenia, Agamemnon's daughter, at the beginning of Euripides' tragedy, of Scout in *To Kill a Mockingbird*, Frankie in *The Member of the Wedding*, Rahel in Arundhati Roy's novel *The God of Small Things* set in India, Tambu in Tsi Tsi Dangaremba's novel *Nervous Conditions* set in Zimbabwe, Claudia in Toni Morrison's *The Bluest Eye* set in Lorraine, Ohio, Jamaica Kincaid's Annie John growing up in Antigua, the voice of Wadjda – a spirited 10-year-old living in Riyadh, Saudi Arabia at a time when women couldn't drive and girls couldn't ride bicycles. In the 2012 film

Wadjda, written and directed by Haifaa al-Mansour –
the first feature film shot entirely in Saudi Arabia, the
first feature-length film made by a Saudi woman director
– 10-year-old Wadjda wants a bicycle, and with the help
of her mother, she gets one. At the end of the film, we
see her riding the green bicycle she'd set her heart on,
racing her friend Abdullah.

The voice is culturally inflected but easily identifiable.
A girl on the threshold of becoming a young woman
sees what she is facing and says what she sees. Like
the small boy in Andersen's fairytale who says that the
emperor is naked. We know this wild voice.

In Charlotte Brontë's novel, when Aunt Reed tells
Jane that "children must be corrected for their faults,"
Jane cries out, "in a savage, high voice," "deceit is not
my fault!"[15] And that is precisely the issue. Honest
and direct, children's voices must be corrected, or dis-
missed as childish, naive or mistaken, stupid or crazy.
Otherwise, what they say would have to be addressed.
Yet once the correction is made or the voice recedes into
silence, few people ask: "Where is that honest voice?"

Millions of readers read Anne Frank's diary without
realizing that they were not reading Anne's actual diary
but rather a version of it that Anne herself had edited.
I include myself among those who, in reading what we
thought was the actual diary, never stopped to ask:
what's missing? The edited voice sounded like Anne's
voice. And after all, Anne had done the editing.

Yet like a fossil preserved in amber, we have Anne's
actual diary. It was rescued by Miep Geis, one of the
Frank family's helpers, who collected the pages of the
actual diary along with Anne's edited version from the
floor of the secret annex after the Nazis had left, saved

them and gave them to Anne's father when he returned from Auschwitz. Rather than being erased or lost to history, Anne's editing of her own voice was preserved, published in an unwieldy "critical edition," where you can see, one beneath the other, three versions of most diary entries (some were lost to history and Anne hadn't quite reached the end of her editing when the Nazis burst into the hideout). But for the most part, we have the diary as Anne actually wrote it, the diary as Anne edited it, and the diary as edited by her father – the version that was first published, the version of the diary that most of us read.

In March 1944, Anne heard on Radio Free Orange, broadcasting from London into the Netherlands, that the Dutch government in exile had plans to set up a war museum after the war. They were interested in diaries, letters, and collections of sermons that would show how the Dutch people carried on their lives under the extreme conditions of the war. Anne's dream was to become a famous writer, and here was her chance. Between May and August 1944, she rewrote more than 300 pages of her diary, with an eye to having it chosen for the museum.

What did she leave out? Her pleasure in her changing body with its "sweet secrets," her awareness of adult hypocrisy, especially when speaking about purity and marriage ("nothing more than eyewash"), and the omission that took me by surprise: she edited out her pleasure with her mother, her closeness with her mother and sister ("Mummy, Margot and I are thick as thieves again"). Anne knew what people expected a "young girl" to know, which feelings and thoughts of hers would be acceptable, and she wanted her diary to be chosen. Her pleasure in her sexuality and her sharp eye for adult hypocrisy were not acceptable, and also her closeness to her mother and sister. Her coldness toward her mother was fine.[16]

The brilliance of dissociation as a response to trauma is that what is dissociated, split off from consciousness, is not lost. Association – the stream of consciousness and the touch of relationship – can unlock dissociation, bringing what had been kept apart from awareness back into consciousness. When this happens, we have the sensation of knowing something that is at once familiar and surprising – something we knew, and yet did not know that we knew.

The research with girls is the centerpiece of the triptych because it was girls narrating their experiences in coming of age who first drew attention to a betrayal of relationship that was culturally sanctioned, in a situation where the stakes were high (identity and inclusion were on the line). Articulate girls named the paradox they were facing: the price of having relationships was to give up on relationship by silencing an honest voice. Therapists working with women have written about this paradoxical sacrifice of relationship for the sake of having relationships,[17] but it was the research on girls' development that showed this sacrifice to be rooted in a process of initiation that is culturally scripted, morally sanctioned, and socially enforced.

The initiation begins with boys. In *When Boys Become Boys* – the first panel of the triptych – Judy Chu records what she came to know by listening to 4- and 5-year-old boys. She saw evidence of boys' resistance to becoming a "boy" in their strategic concealment of their empathy and desire for closeness. Countering common descriptions of boys as relationally obtuse, she records boys' relational astuteness. Their relational capacities are not lost, Chu writes. "Rather, boys' socialization toward cultural constructions of masculinity that are defined in opposition to femininity seems mainly to force a split between what boys know (e.g. about themselves, their relationships, and their world) and what boys show."[18]

Winning the boys' trust, Chu learns about The Mean Team – "a club created by the boys, for the boys, and for the stated purpose of acting against the girls." The Mean Team established a masculinity defined in opposition to and as the opposite of a femininity associated with being good and nice. Thus, the main activity of The Mean Team was, in the words of one of the boys, "to bother people."[19]

Chu observes that the very relational capacities boys learn to shield in becoming a "boy," the empathy and emotional sensitivity that enable them to read the human world around them so accurately and so astutely, are essential if they are to realize the closeness they now seek with other boys. Yet in blunting or concealing these capacities in order to establish themselves as one of the boys, they render that closeness unattainable.

Writing from the vantage point of middle age, as an epilogue to his book *Thirteen Ways of Looking at a Man*, the psychoanalyst Donald Moss recalls the initiation that Chu witnesses.[20] He was in the first grade and it was his turn to lead the class in singing the song that, of all the songs they had learned that year, was his favorite (which the children were to have kept secret). There was no question in Moss's mind as to which song he would choose. The song he loved, "the most beautiful song I had heard," was the lullaby from *Hansel and*

Gretel, "When at night I go to sleep, fourteen angels watch do keep." Yet seeing the shock in the eyes of the boys in the first row when he starts to say "the lullaby," he quickly reverses direction. "Just kidding," he says. His favorite song, he tells them, the one he will lead the class in singing, is the Marines' hymn, "From the halls of Montezuma to the shores of Tripoli."

To Moss, this was an act of "treachery." He had betrayed his angels, been "unfaithful" to them; he had "renounced them in public and continued to do so for many years." The residue, he writes, was "a melancholia, tied to the boy's awareness" that "what he is 'really' doing in that fateful turning outward is simultaneously preserving and betraying his original love of angels, affirming and denying his new love of boys." In this betrayal of what's right, "he and the boys are joined together in looking elsewhere for the angels they might have all once had."[21]

The moral injury was a betrayal of love.

3. The Love Laws

In an overlooked passage, midway through Tolstoy's novel *Anna Karenina*, we hear the hushed voice of Karenin: "[P]rior to the day when he saw his dying wife, he had not known his own heart."[22] Like Hawthorne in *The Scarlet Letter*, Tolstoy takes us into the territory of the Love Laws – Arundhati Roy's term for the laws that establish "who should be loved. And how. And how much."[23]

In Hawthorne's novel, the word "patriarchy" appears repeatedly – "patriarchal personage," "patriarchal privilege," "patriarchal deacon" – along with a portrait of "the father of the Custom-House, the patriarch," who "had no soul, no heart, no mind." He resembles Karenin, also a government official.[24]

The central characters, Anna Karenina and Hester Prynne, are so dazzling that our eye fixes on them. These vibrant women stand out among the "Goodwives," who are gray and muted by comparison. Anna and Hester break the Love Laws, driven by a "lawless passion." We want to know what happens to them. It is almost as if they serve as decoys, to distract us from what Tolstoy and Hawthorne are showing us about the costs that patriarchy exacts on men. The names of Hawthorne's central male characters – Dimmesdale and Chillingworth – give us a clue. Yet Hester's scarlet A so rivets our attention that we may miss what these names convey: a man of nature – Mr. Dale – has become dim, and a man of worth has become chilling. How did this happen?

Tolstoy takes us to the core. Anna is due to give birth to the child she conceived with her lover, Vronsky. Deathly ill, she sends a telegram to her husband, begging him to come and to forgive her so she can die in peace. He assumes it's a trick and feels only contempt; yet he is concerned that if he doesn't go and she dies, it would "not only be cruel – and everybody would condemn me – but it would be stupid on my part."[25] So he goes.

Readers often forget or don't quite take in that at this juncture in Tolstoy's novel, Karenin offers Anna both her freedom and her son. He will divorce her and, by taking the disgrace upon himself, make it possible for her to go out into society and to keep Seryozha with her.

As it turns out, Anna does not take the offer.

Her decision is unexplained. In a novel where we are told even what the dog thinks, Anna's refusal to take her freedom, which seals her fate, is conveyed cryptically in a terse, one-sentence paragraph: "A month later, Alexei Alexandrovich was left alone in his apartment with his son, and Anna went abroad with Vronsky without obtaining a divorce and resolutely abandoning the idea."[26]

We are, however, told in detail what happened to Karenin. "At his wife's bedside he had given himself for the first time in his life to that feeling of tender compassion which other people's suffering evoked in him, and which he had previously been ashamed of as a bad weakness."

> [He] suddenly felt not only relief from his suffering but also an inner peace that he had never experienced before. He suddenly felt that the very thing that had once been the source of his suffering had become the source of his spiritual joy, that what had seemed insoluble when he condemned, reproached, and hated, became simple and clear when he forgave and loved.[27]

Anna doesn't die. Karenin forgives Vronsky. He tells him:

> You may trample me in the mud, make me the laughing stock of society, I will not abandon her. I will never say a word of reproach to you ... My duty is clearly ordained for me: I must be with her and I will be. If she wishes to see you, I will let you know.[28]

Why did this passage surprise me? I had read the novel several times and yet had no memory of this change in Karenin. I did not recall that he offered Anna both her freedom and Seryozha, or that she, given the opportunity to have what she had wanted – a divorce and her son – had "resolutely abandoned the idea."[29] I had to ask what was my investment in viewing Karenin as simply cold and heartless, and seeing Anna's tragedy as inescapable? What had kept me from taking in the words on the page? Because what I overlooked could not have been more clearly stated.

Karenin settles into the household and begins for the first time to observe the people around him, the wet nurse, the governess, and his son. He regrets that he hadn't paid much attention to Seryozha. Now he "stroked the boy's hair with his hand." For the newborn little girl, "he had some special feeling, not only of pity but also of tenderness ... he did not notice how he came to love her." He looked after her so she would not die; he "went to the nursery several times a day and sat there for a long while," watching her closely. "He would sometimes spend half an hour silently gazing at the saffron-red, downy and wrinkled little face of the sleeping baby," and "felt utterly at peace and in harmony with himself, and saw nothing extraordinary in his situation, nothing that needed to be changed."[30]

But . . .

the more time passed, the more clearly he saw that, natural as this situation was for him now, he would not be allowed to remain in it. He felt that, besides the good spiritual force that guided his soul, there was another force, crude and equally powerful, if not more so, that guided his life, and that this force would not give him the humble peace he desired. He felt that everybody looked at him with questioning surprise, not understanding him and expecting something from him.[31]

Over a stretch of fifteen pages, Tolstoy repeats his description of this force that guided Karenin's life – crude force, powerful force, mysterious force – as if to make sure it stays in our mind, like Vronsky's strong, white teeth. In the face of this force, Karenin feels powerless. "He knew beforehand that everything was against him and that he would not be allowed to do what now seemed to him so natural and good, but would be forced to do what was bad but seemed to them the proper thing."[32]

What seemed to Karenin "natural and good" was, in the eyes of the world, bad and improper. A crude, powerful, mysterious force that was "contrary to his inner mood guided his life, demanding the carrying out of its will." It caused him to feel ashamed of "that feeling of tender compassion which other people's suffering evoked in him" and to regard it as a "bad weakness."

We learn that Karenin had been an orphan, his childhood bleak. His pursuit of status and honor can be seen as an attempt to fill that void. He was a man afraid of feeling, cut off from love, ashamed of his humanity. Until suddenly – also a repeated word in this passage – his heart opens.

He writes to Anna, "Tell me yourself what will give you true happiness and peace in your soul. I give myself over entirely to your will and your sense of justice."[33] Suddenly they are complete human beings – Karenin with feelings of tender compassion, Anna with a will and a sense of justice.

But the world is ruled by a crude force. Karenin knew that he would "be forced to do what was bad." The betrayal of what's right is seemingly inescapable, and yet a confusion has set in because what he had considered a bad weakness and shameful now seemed to him natural and good. We are not told why Anna abandons the idea of obtaining a divorce and having her son with her. Only that she does.

We know that this story cannot end well.

5

In a Different Voice:
Act II

I am flying home from a family vacation and among the films available for viewing is Paul Thomas Anderson's *Phantom Thread*, starring Daniel Day-Lewis. I decide to watch it. I don't recall ever feeling so disquieted by a film, so destabilized by the responses it evokes in me. I am tempted to stop watching. The film is cueing me to respond in a way that I recognize and find familiar, and then undercutting that response. I leave the plane feeling irritated and unsettled.

The following week I teach a master class in Brussels, and on the return flight *Phantom Thread* is still playing. For reasons I don't quite understand – it could just be Daniel Day-Lewis – I feel compelled to watch it again. But this time I know what I am seeing and my response becomes one of astonishment. That this film was made, that it is being shown on a plane, and that it was made by a straight man – this all strikes me as deeply hopeful. When my husband asks why his being straight is relevant, I can't explain it. But by then I have two further examples of films released within the same year that were written and directed by straight men – Paul Schrader's *First Reformed* and Spike Lee's *BlacKkKlansman* – films that I recognize as harbingers. To me they signal the opening of a new act in the drama of *In a Different Voice* – one where we witness the audacity of love and of caring.

1. Paul Thomas Anderson: *Phantom Thread*

In an interview with Terry Gross on *Fresh Air*, Anderson, who lives with the actor and comedian Maya Rudolph (who starred on *Saturday Night Live*), says that the inspiration for *Phantom Thread* came from his own experience. The incident in question occurred when he became ill with a flu so severe that it became impossible for him to do what he always had done, namely, to "soldier on." Forced to slow down, with no choice but to take to his bed, he needed his partner to take care of him, and she did. Yet he was taken aback when she said, "Oh, I like you like this," meaning, he explains, vulnerable and open. To him, this was a revelation.[1]

In the film, Reynolds Woodcock (Day-Lewis) is a renowned fashion designer who makes gowns for wealthy women and royalty. He is elegant and handsome, a self-obsessed man, consumed by his talent. Day-Lewis worked closely with Anderson in creating the script; like Anderson, he too is in a long relationship with a strong woman, the filmmaker Rebecca Miller. As fathers of sons, both men can be said to be invested, or at the very least implicated, in what it means and what it takes to become a man.

As the film opens, we see Woodcock deliver an elaborate gown to one of his fawning wealthy patrons.

Exhausted, he drives to the country that evening. In the morning, he goes to a small country inn for breakfast, and there he meets Alma (the name means soul), a waitress. She stumbles and blushes as she approaches his table and we register his attraction; he sees something in her and invites her to dine with him that evening. But, as we also see, Alma sees him. On the paper she hands him with her number, she has written, "For the hungry boy."

What follows is predictable: Alma becomes Reynolds's muse, his model, and his lover – the latest in the string of women who entice him, whom he picks up and then discards when he finds them tiresome, or irritating, or when they become a distraction and disrupt his routine. Because, as him name conveys, Woodcock is a rigid man. This doesn't stop Alma from asserting herself. Right at the start, she tells him that, in a staring contest, she will win, and it's true: in the end her gaze is the more unwavering.

The phantom thread that runs through the film – we glimpse it briefly at the outset, lose sight of it, and then see it again at the end – is that Alma is the film's protagonist. The story is her story about Reynolds. At the opening and closing frames of the film, we see her telling it to the man who, in the course of the film, we will come to know as the doctor. She is the protagonist also in the sense that she initiates the action upon which the plot of the film turns – the action that leads Terry Gross to ask Anderson: "Do you sanction what she does?"

This is the unsettling question, the ethical question. "I'm groovy," Anderson says. He sanctions love, he explains. And then adds that Reynolds "sees something in her . . . he's never seen before in someone," that "he's responding to a kind of audacity in her that he finds really attractive," and that when it comes right down to it, it takes a "gigantic and large act . . . for him to feel dominated and cared about," an act that "brings him back to this love that he clearly has for her." This is the unsettling insight.

In one sense it's obvious. As long as Reynolds remains rigid and in control, he can neither feel nor express his love. What's not obvious at first is that it takes an audacious act on Alma's part to release what otherwise remains imprisoned: Reynolds's heart, and more specifically his love for her. Audacious in the sense of involving risk and also in forcing him to relinquish control. Here is what I think makes Anderson's (and his proxy Reynolds's) straightness relevant: because, as a straight man, he has, one could say, everything to gain by staying in control and maintaining his position of dominance. And besides, audacity is not a word we commonly associate with love and caring.

I want to pause for a moment to register Anderson's use of the word "care" in this context and his linking of Alma's caring about Reynolds to her taking control and dominating him. Reynolds would never let go of control, would never allow himself to become vulnerable, and thus could not access his love or allow himself to feel cared about by her. In the course of the film, Reynolds comes both to recognize and to sanction what she does, and, in the end, it is this that makes Anderson's film at once so extraordinary and so challenging.

Let's go on. Alma sees that Reynolds's interest in her is waning. He is irritated by the noise she makes at breakfast when she butters her toast. She counters that this is his problem, but, as he said to her predecessor,

"I cannot start my day with a confrontation. I simply have no time for confrontations." We see the writing on the wall: Reynolds is preparing to send Alma away. His sister Cyril will do the dirty work for him, sending her off with a dress as compensation.

Anticipating this move, Alma decides to take matters into her own hands. She will prepare a romantic dinner for just the two of them. She will make him a martini, cook him asparagus, and in that way show him her love. Cyril is wary and tries to warn her, but Alma goes ahead with her plan, which explodes in her face. Reynolds is furious, an icy fury. She has disrupted his routine and, besides, she did not make the asparagus in the way that he likes. "Are you a special agent sent here to ruin my evening and possibly my entire life?" he asks her. "When the hell did this happen? Who are you? Do you have a gun?"

She tells him that she could not bear just standing around waiting for him to send her away. Her position was untenable. We see this, but Reynolds is unmoved. Silently we tell her: leave him!

It's not what she does. Instead, she sees what he cannot allow her to see and she acts on what she perceives: not only is Reynolds a hungry boy, he is a loving man living behind a barricade of constriction, a man caught in a kind of elegant captivity. Facing his impending rejection of her, Alma recognizes that his love had become captive, not only to the ghost of his dead mother but also to his rigid masculinity. Identifying the toxin, she finds the antidote.

The film takes on the quality of a fairytale as we watch Alma go into the woods. In his interview with Terry Gross, Anderson explains that he had been reading ghost stories and also fairytales, which, given his four young children, were lying around the house. We see Alma in the kitchen poring over a book of mushrooms, peering at the illustrations. We watch her in the woods picking a yellow-brown mushroom we recognize as poisonous. We see her scrape its flesh and carefully measure out the grains. She is making a tea for Reynolds. We see him become violently ill.

Do you sanction what she does?

In a scene after his submission to the illness, Reynolds, wearing a woolen bathrobe over his pajamas, sits with Alma on the sofa where she had spent the night. Now for the first time he says what previously he could not say. He tells Alma that he loves her. He asks her: will she marry him? We watch her seeing him, a long look. She has to be clear about what she is seeing. Yes, she says. Yes, she will.

Do you sanction what she does?

The story has a fairytale ending. Alma and Reynolds have a baby. They are in a park. Cyril, Reynolds's sister, sits on a bench; we see her rocking the baby carriage as Reynolds and Alma walk down a path together. But all this is narrated by Alma. Sitting in an armchair and speaking to the doctor, she tells him about Reynolds and the life they have created together. It is a life of abundance that encompasses them both, including his devotion to work and also her love of play. It was not the romantic dinner but the poisonous mushroom that was the crucial intervention. An antidote found in nature to something toxic in the culture, an audacious act at once risky and freeing, releasing love from a manhood that imprisoned it.

2. Paul Schrader: *First Reformed*

Paul Schrader cites Ingmar Bergman's *Winter Light* among the inspirations for his film *First Reformed*, which also centers on a pastor who has lost his faith. The pastor is Ernst Toller, and Schrader makes the connection to Donne: "Never send to know for whom the bell tolls, it tolls for thee." It could be the slogan of the environmental movement, which features centrally in the film. Schrader explains that he made the film because, having reached his seventies, he told himself, "It's time to write that script you swore you would never write."[2]

A member of a military family, Toller had been a chaplain at Virginia Military Institute. He encouraged his son to enlist in the Marines, but when his son is killed in the Iraq War, Toller is shattered. His faith is challenged, and he leaves the military academy; he leaves his marriage. He becomes the pastor at First Reformed, a church that is a historic relic, now mainly a tourist attraction, an adjunct to a thriving megachurch with its ebullient Black pastor.

Toller sells postcards from the gift shop. He conducts services for the scatter of people who show up on Sundays. And among them one Sunday is a pale young woman who waits for him after the service. She is pregnant. Her name is Mary. She explains that her husband insists that she cannot have the baby. Will Reverend Toller speak with him?

Toller drives to the house to find the husband glued to his computer. He blizzards the reverend with chart after chart forecasting environmental disaster. How could one think of bringing a child into this? "Can God forgive us for what we've done to this world?" he asks.

Toller has no answer. "Who can know the mind of God?" he says.

The husband goes into the woods and shoots himself. Toller finds the body. When the megachurch pastor organizes a celebration to mark the sestercentennial of First Reformed, which is underwritten by a fossil fuel company, it becomes clear: Toller has reached the end of his rope. As we watch the crowd assemble in the historic church for the celebration, we see Toller in his upstairs room retrieving the explosive vest he had taken from the environmentalist's home. We watch him strap it on under his vestments. He opens a bottle of Drano and pours himself a cup.

In an interview, Schrader speaks about the ending:

> He drank the cup of [Drano], and now he's there dying. And God comes – this is the God that hasn't spoken to him for the whole movie – and as he's on all fours dying, God walks over to him and says, "Reverend Toller, would you like to see what heaven looks like? I'm going to show it to you right now. I'm going to open the doors and this is what it looks like. It looks like one, long, slow kiss." And he's in heaven.

"It's an unexpected moment," Schrader explains, "that leaves you thinking, whoa, what did I just watch?"

What we see is that Mary is with him. Suddenly she's there in the room with Toller, and they experience the full force of their love and it releases him. We don't quite know if what we are watching is happening in that spare room with its white walls and wooden floor, winter light coming in through the windows, or in Toller's mind as he is dying, or whether they are in fact in heaven, and in the end it doesn't matter. Because Schrader has made a film to show that in the face of impending doom, there is only one answer: love. Schrader believed it but he'd sworn he'd never say it.

3. Spike Lee: *BlacKkKlansman*

BlacKkKlansman. The title stops me, and then I see it. Spike Lee is taking us into the heartland of white supremacy, the KKK, but the second k is also a bridge, crossing the gap between Black and Klansman. A Black Klansman? It actually happened. In the 1970s, in Colorado Springs, Ron Stallworth became the Jackie Robinson of the Colorado Springs police, as the chief described him, the first Black man to join the force. Becoming a detective, he then went undercover and joined the Klan. Improbable but true.

In Lee's retelling, here's how it happens. An ad in the local paper says that the Klan is seeking recruits. Stallworth picks up the phone and dials the number. "God bless White America," he says in the message he leaves on the machine. By mistake, he also leaves his real name. The Klan calls right back. They have no inkling who they are talking to. Fluent in jive and also the King's English, Stallworth code-switches. But when they say they want to meet him, Ron Stallworth needs a white face. In Lee's film, the white cop who stands in for Stallworth undercover is Flip Zimmerman, a Jew.

I see the film at a movie theater in Oak Bluffs, the largely African American summer community on the otherwise mostly white island of Martha's Vineyard, originally inhabited by the Wampanoags, Native Americans. I register my unease as I watch the opening, a scene from *Gone with the Wind,* showing Scarlett

O'Hara weaving her way through the bodies of dead and wounded Confederate soldiers lying on the streets of Atlanta, followed by grainy black and white shots of a pro-segregationist stumbling through a monologue in which he explains the so-called science behind white supremacy. Yet part way into the actual story, when the Black Ron Stallworth asks his Jewish white counterpart Flip Zimmerman, "Why you acting like you ain't got skin in the game?" my unease vanishes.

It was Lee's decision to make the white cop Jewish (in Stallworth's memoir he is not), and it strikes me initially as a courageous move on Lee's part, given the tensions between Blacks and Jews. I come to see it as part of a larger pattern, whereby Lee challenges what he calls the "Okey-dokey," things we unwittingly nod our assent to. And I recognize that especially now – when in Lee's words we as a nation are living in "pure, undiluted insanity" – his film, as he explains to a journalist, is directed to America and asking: "Why don't you wake up?'

Why you acting like you ain't got skin in the game?

In *BlacKkKlansman*, Lee casts the debate over violence versus nonviolent responses to the violence of racism as an argument between the glorious Patrice, head of the Black Students Union at Colorado College, and Stallworth, the undercover cop. Patrice hosts the rally for the Black Panther leader Stokely Carmichael: she introduces Carmichael by his *nom de guerre* Kwame Ture; she raises her fist in the air in the call for Black power; to her all cops are "pigs." Stallworth is drawn to Patrice, he raises his fist in half-hearted assent to her message, but he is attending the rally as the detective assigned to ferret out and prevent outbreaks of violence.

And it is Stallworth, working undercover with the Klan, who in the end saves Patrice from the bomb that was meant to kill her – the bomb that had been planted by the wife of one of the Klansmen. Black/white, Black/Jew, man/woman – none of these binaries goes unchallenged.

Lee released his film in the summer of 2018, on the first anniversary of the Charlottesville rally. He had ended it with footage from Charlottesville showing swastika-carrying white supremacists marching, and this was followed by a photograph of Heather Heyer, the white woman killed by the white supremacist who plowed his car into the counter-protestors.

"Maybe not everyone who is white is a racist," Lee says to one of the journalists who question him, "but racism is what makes us white."[3] Maybe not every man is a patriarch, but patriarchy is what makes us men. Like Anderson and Schrader, Lee is a straight man; he too is in a long relationship with a strong woman, Tonya Lewis Lee, film and television producer, writer and advocate for women and children's health. He too is the father of a son. However starkly the words "Black" and "Klan" stand out, "man" is also part of his title. And in his film, it is Ron Stallworth, the Black Klansman, who takes a stand against a manhood predicated on white supremacy, a manhood shored up by violence.

Among the deepest insights I have come to in the course of my work is that the requisites for love and the requisites for citizenship in a democratic society are one and the same. Both depend on our having a voice, the ability to communicate our experience, and on our desire to live in relationship, not alone or walled off in silence. With the paradigm shift that has been spreading through the human sciences since the mid-1970s, we can ask new questions about both ethics and politics, because, as the evidence now attests, we, meaning humans, are inherently relational and responsive beings, born with a voice and with the desire to engage responsively with others. It no longer makes sense to ask how we gain our humanity. Instead, the question becomes: How do we lose it?

What struck me as hopeful in 2018, along with the unprecedented number and diversity of women elected to the House of Representatives in the mid-term election, was that three straight men, filmmakers working in the mainstream, had taken up the challenge set down by *In a Different Voice*: namely, the need for a human voice to counter a patriarchal voice that constrains our humanity. They take up the call to reframe the understanding of care and take it a step further by recognizing the audacity in caring and the risk it involves: the audacity of love.

In a Different Voice: Act II: What initially sounded like a woman's story can now be recognized as a human story (*Why are you acting like you ain't got skin in the game, brother?*); the different voice is a voice that helps by opposing; it is a voice of resistance, deeply unsettling (*Do you sanction what she does?*), leaving us unsure as to what we're watching (*Is this love happening in real time, or is it a fantasy?*) and improbably crossing what had been taken as irreconcilable opposites or impermeable boundaries: Black and white, Black and Jewish, man and woman, masculine and feminine, militant and nonviolent, audacious and caring.

Epilogue

The Ethic of Care

It's fifty years since John Berger wrote, "Never again will a single story be told as though it's the only one." It's forty years since *In a Different Voice* recast the conversation about self and morality as a conversation about voice and relationship. And it's twenty-five years since Arundhati Roy coined the phrase "Love Laws" for the laws that set down who should be loved (and how and how much).[1]

I gather up what I have come to know. The different voice (the voice of care ethics) is a human voice. The betrayal of relationship is a betrayal of what's right. The ethic of care is an ethic of resistance to moral injury. The Love Laws are a mainstay of patriarchy.

When I first typed the word "voice" on a sheet of yellow paper in the winter of 1975, it was to record "a distinctive voice" – distinctive in "the different perspective it brings to bear on the construction and resolution of moral problems." I had been listening to women, and it was women's voices that brought this difference to my attention. I didn't think of the voice as a women's voice, and yet it sounded "feminine."

Recently I was asked to talk about my experience in writing *In a Different Voice*. Going over what for me was familiar ground, I was surprised to arrive at an insight about something that had been confusing me for many years. It occurred to me that I had inadvertently built a tension into the title of both my initial essay, "In a Different Voice: Women's Conceptions of Self and of Morality" (1977), and the book that followed, *In a Different Voice: Psychological Theory and Women's Development* (1982). I had joined an exploration of difference (a different voice – different from what?) with the subject of women, thus setting myself up for a trap that it has taken me years to extricate myself from: Are women different? Are women different from men? Do women make a difference? Am I an essentialist? Do I know that all women are not the same? Do I know that race and class matter as much as or even more than sex or gender? And so on. Ironically, my work came to be viewed through the lens of the very binary comparisons and hierarchies that I had set out to challenge.

It was the studies with girls that brought the subject of patriarchy to the fore. Patriarchy, with its paradox of forcing a sacrifice of relationship for the sake of having relationships. Patriarchy, with its gender binaries and hierarchies forcing splits in the psyche. Tolstoy was right. There is a force. Crude, powerful, and mysterious – his adjectives all apply. This force turns something that seems natural and good into something that is deemed bad and improper. In Tolstoy's novel, Karenin is helpless in the face of this force. But in the studies of development that began in the 1980s and continued through the 1990s and into the current century, my colleagues and I saw children resist this force and this resistance was associated with psychological resilience.

In the resisting injustice seminar, a Black law student from Brooklyn names loneliness as the price she paid for saying what she thought. She had to be willing to lose relationships in order to put them to the test. The loneliness was painful but in the end she concludes it was worth it to hold out for real relationship.

It is a late afternoon in early September, the beginning of the school year. We are only starting to know one another. The word "loneliness" lingers, emotionally resonant. The atmosphere in the seminar room shifts; everyone is attentive. A white law student wearing a sweatshirt from a fish store in Massachusetts recalls the moment when she decided she would no longer maintain relationships by not saying what she felt and thought.

I listen intently, moved by the clarity of these women's awareness of choices they made around speaking and not speaking. I am moved especially by a woman naming loneliness as the price she paid for saying what she thought. Because I had done that – I had said what I thought – I remembered saying it – I remembered deciding to say it – and I had felt the loneliness after losing the friendship.

Women's voices have always been at the center of my work, often speaking in counterpoint to the voice of psychological or moral theory. At a certain point, the voices of girls took over, speaking about relationships and resisting a voice that carried patriarchal authority: "Sorry," 12-year-old Neeti says, "but he's only seven . . . people are more important than rules."

She is speaking about her homesick cousin, talking to the camp director who had made a rule against calling home.[2]

What strikes me about girls is that they are in our midst. Across time and cultures, from Euripides to Toni Morrison, artists have heard the voices of girls as a voice of resistance. It is a voice we know and yet we continue to find it surprising because this is not how we usually think about girls.

Boys also are in our midst and they too surprise us. In *Close*, a 2022 film written and directed by the Belgian filmmaker Lukas Dhont, we witness the emotional closeness of two 13-year-old boys. And then we see what happens when their closeness is questioned: "Are you a couple?" they are asked. Suddenly manhood is on the line. The film won the *Grand Prix* at Cannes, and Dhont explained that in writing the film, he was inspired by Niobe Way's book *Deep Secrets*, by her studies of teenage boys' friendships. He named his film "Close" after "close friendship," a term Way uses repeatedly.

I find myself asking what stands in the way of our seeing what is right in front of our eyes and listening to voices that are in our midst? What investment do we have in not hearing girls' voices as courageous, or recognizing girls' resistance as a healthy resistance, or not seeing the emotional intimacy of boys' friendships or recognizing boys' tenderness and emotional intelligence? I find these questions painful, in part because I know the costs of not seeing and not listening, the price of carelessness and indifference. I know that morality and gender scripts can blind us to the obvious. And keep us from hearing what is surprisingly accessible. I know that if you want to hear the under-voice – the human voice that goes undercover – you may have to question the cover voice:

> *If it's good to be empathic with people and responsive to people's needs and concerns, why is it "selfish" to respond to yourself?*
>
> *Why is that the ultimate nightmare [her in the arms of another man]?*
>
> *Is that true?*
>
> *Do you believe that?*
>
> *Do you really feel that way?*

As an ethics of relationship, care ethics is a guide to knowing others and oneself. It is a guide to listening. Its wisdom is a psychological wisdom: notice what happens when you replace judgment with curiosity.

From the vantage point of the present, then, it has become possible for me to clarify and articulate what couldn't quite be seen or said at the time when my work was first published: that the "different voice" (the voice of care ethics), although initially heard as a "feminine" voice, is in fact a human voice, that the voice it differs from is a patriarchal voice (listen for the tell-tale gender binaries and hierarchies), and that where patriarchy is in force and enforced, the human voice is a voice of resistance, and care ethics is an ethics of liberation.

With this theoretical clarification, it becomes evident why *In a Different Voice* continues to resonate strongly with people's experience and, perhaps more crucially, why the different voice is a voice for the twenty-first century.

Acknowledgments

Chapter 3 appeared in an earlier form as "Disrupting the Story: Enter Eve" in the *Journal of the American Psychoanalytic Association* 68(4), pp. 675–693. Copyright © 2020 by the American Psychoanalytic Association. Reprinted by permission of SAGE Publications Inc.

Chapter 4 appeared in an earlier form as "Moral Injury and the Ethic of Care: Reframing the Conversation about Differences" in the *Journal of Social Philosophy* 45(1), pp. 89–106, Spring 2014. Reprinted by permission of Wiley Periodicals, Inc.

Chapter 5 appeared in an earlier form as "'In a Different Voice': Act II" in the *Los Angeles Review of Books*, March 15, 2019. Reprinted by permission of the *LARB*.

Notes

Introduction

1 S. Freud, "Some Psychical Consequences of the Anatomical Distinction Between the Sexes" (1925), in *Standard Edition of the Complete Psychological Works of Sigmund Freud*, Vol. XIX, trans. and ed. James Strachey (London: Hogarth Press, 1961); L. Kohlberg and R. Kramer, "Continuities and Discontinuities in Child and Adult Moral Development," *Human Development* 12 (1969), pp. 93–120; E. H. Erikson, *Identity: Youth and Crisis* (New York: Norton, 1968); J. Piaget, *The Moral Judgment of the Child* (New York: The Free Press, 1932).

2 C. Gilligan, "In a Different Voice: Women's Conceptions of Self and of Morality," *Harvard Educational Review* 47/4 (1977), pp. 481–517; C. Gilligan, *In a Different Voice: Psychological Theory and Women's Development* (Cambridge, MA: Harvard University Press, 1982).

3 V. Woolf, *A Room of One's Own* (New York: Harcourt, 2021[1929]).

4 bell hooks, *Talking Back: Thinking Feminist, Thinking Black* (New York: Routledge, 2015).

5 S. Ferenczi, "Confusion of Tongues between Adults and the Child: The Language of Tenderness and of Passion," *Contemporary Psychoanalysis* 24 (1988[1933]), pp. 196–206.

6 M. Garcia, *We Are Not Born Submissive: How Patriarchy Shapes Women's Lives* (Princeton, NJ: Princeton University Press, 2021).

7 C. Gilligan and J. Attanucci, "Two Moral Orientations: Gender Differences and Similarities," *Merrill-Palmer Quarterly* 34/3 (1988), pp. 223–237.

8 C. Gilligan and G. Wiggins, "The Origins of Morality in Early Childhood Relationships," in J. Kagan and S. Lamb (eds.), *The Emergence of Morality in Young Children* (Chicago, IL: University of Chicago Press, 1987), pp. 277–305.

9 L. M. Brown and C. Gilligan, *Meeting at the Crossroads: Women's Psychology and Girls' Development* (Cambridge, MA: Harvard University Press, 1992).

10 C. Gilligan, "Joining the Resistance: Psychology and Politics, Girls and Women," *Michigan Quarterly Review* 24 (1990), pp. 501–536; see also C. Gilligan, *Joining the Resistance* (Cambridge, UK: Polity Press, 2011).

11 N. Way, *Deep Secrets: Boys' Friendships and the Crisis of Connection* (Cambridge, MA: Harvard University Press, 2011).

12 A. Damasio, *Descartes' Error: Emotion, Reason, and the Human Brain* (New York: Putnam, 1994).

13 J. Herman, *Trauma and Recovery* (New York: Basic Books, 1992).

14 C. Gilligan, "The Centrality of Relationships in Human

Development: A Puzzle, Some Evidence, and a Theory," in K. Fischer and G. Noam (eds.), *Development and Vulnerability in Close Relationships* (Mahwah, NJ: Lawrence Erlbaum, 1996).

15 S. Nolen-Hoeksema, J. S. Girgus, and M. E. Seligman, "Sex Differences in Depression and Explanatory Style in Children," *Journal of Youth and Adolescence* 20/2 (1991), pp. 233–245.

16 M. H. Kingston, *The Woman Warrior: Memoirs of a Girlhood among Ghosts* (New York: Alfred A. Knopf, 1976).

17 According to *The Girls' Index,* a large-scale national survey of more than 10,000 girls designed to develop a deeper understanding of teenage girls throughout the US, 46% of the participants reported that they don't say what they are thinking, or disagree with others because they want to be liked. That percentage rises to 62% for girls with a GPA above 4.0, indicating that using traditional measures of success, the highest achieving girls in the US are the most concerned with the outside approval of others.

18 C. Gilligan, *The Birth of Pleasure* (New York: Knopf, 2002).

19 See C. Gilligan and D. A. J. Richards, *The Deepening Darkness: Patriarchy, Resistance, and Democracy's Future* (New York: Cambridge University Press, 2008); also, C. Gilligan and D. A. J. Richards, *Darkness Now Visible: Patriarchy's Resurgence and Feminist Resistance* (New York: Cambridge University Press, 2018).

20 See Gilligan, *The Birth of Pleasure*; C. Gilligan and N. Snider, *Why Does Patriarchy Persist?* (Cambridge, UK: Polity, 2018); N. Way, A. Ali, C. Gilligan, and

P. Noguera (eds.), *The Crisis of Connection: Roots, Consequences, and Solutions* (New York: NYU Press, 2018).

21 A. Roy, *The God of Small Things* (New York: Random House, 2017[1997]), p. 168.

22 S. B. Hrdy, *Mothers and Others: The Evolutionary Origins of Mutual Understanding* (Cambridge, MA: Harvard University Press, 2009), p. 287.

23 See Brown and Gilligan, *Meeting at the Crossroads*, pp. 61–62.

24 Herman, *Trauma and Recovery*, p. 7.

Chapter 1: Women's Voices and Women's Silences

1 Joan Morgan, review of Kyla Schuller, *The Trouble with White Women: A Counterhistory of Feminism*, *The New York Times Sunday Book Review*, November 28, 2021, p. 16. A version of the review appeared online in October 2021: https://www.nytimes.com/2021/10/05/books/review/kyla-schuller-the-trouble-with-white-women-a-counterhistory-of-feminism.html.

2 R. Igielnik, S. Keeter, and H. Hartig, "Behind Biden's 2020 Victory: An Examination of the 2020 Electorate Based on Validated Voters," Pew Research Center Report, June 30, 2021.

3 For a more extensive analysis of Iphigenia's resistance, see T. Hartman and C. Buckholtz, "'But I Grieve for My Mother': The Betrayal of Iphigenia and Isaac," in *Are You Not a Man of God? Devotion, Betrayal, and Social Criticism in Jewish Tradition* (New York: Oxford University Press, 2014).

4 Aristotle, *Poetics* (New York: Penguin, 1997[350 BCE]).

5 Margaret Sullivan, "By Bearing Witness – and Hitting

'Record' – 17-year-old Darnella Frazier May Have Changed the World," *The Washington Post*, April 20, 2021.

6 Transcript: Greta Thunberg's speech at the UN Climate Action Summit, September 23, 2019.

7 J. Adelson, *Handbook of Adolescent Psychology* (New York: Wiley, 1980).

8 See Gilligan, "Joining the Resistance: Psychology, Politics, Girls and Women," *Michigan Quarterly Review* 24 (1990), pp. 501–536; C. Gilligan, "Teaching Shakespeare's Sister: Notes from the Underground of Female Adolescence," *Women's Studies Quarterly* 19 (1991), pp. 31–51; C. Gilligan, N. Lyons, and T. Hanmer (eds.), *Making Connections: The Relational Worlds of Adolescent Girls at Emma Willard School* (Cambridge, MA: Harvard University Press, 1989); C. Gilligan, A. G. Rogers, and D. Tolman (eds.), *Women, Girls, and Psychotherapy: Reframing Resistance* (New York: Haworth Press, 1991); L. M. Brown and C. Gilligan, *Meeting at the Crossroads: Women's Psychology and Girls' Development* (Cambridge, MA: Harvard University Press, 1992); J. M. Taylor, C. Gilligan, and A. Sullivan, *Between Voice and Silence: Women and Girls, Race and Relationship* (Cambridge, MA: Harvard University Press, 1995); C. Gilligan, "Remembering Iphigenia: Voice, Resonance, and a Talking Cure," in E. Shapiro (ed.), *The Inner World in the Outer World* (New Haven, CT: Yale University Press, 1996); C. Gilligan, A. G. Rogers, and N. Noel. "Cartography of a Lost Time: Mapping the Crisis of Connection," in N. Way, A. Ali, C. Gilligan, and P. Noguera (eds.), *The Crisis of Connection: Roots, Consequences,*

and Solutions (New York: NYU Press, 2018), pp. 65–88.

9 Rosa Parks was chosen by Montgomery's Black leaders to be the face of the Montgomery bus boycott because, although Colvin was the pioneer, by the time of the court proceedings, the teenager was pregnant and, as Parks explained, she would have been called a "bad girl" by the white press and "her case wouldn't have had a chance."

10 Judy Y. Chu, *When Boys Become Boys: Development, Relationships, and Masculinity* (New York: NYU Press, 2014).

11 N. Way, *Deep Secrets: Boys' Friendships and the Crisis of Connection* (Cambridge, MA: Harvard University Press, 2011), p. 242.

12 The Radical Listening Project, NYU, https://wp.nyu.edu/radicallisteningproject; C. Gilligan and J. Eddy, "The Listening Guide: Replacing Judgment with Curiosity," *Qualitative Psychology* 8/2 (2021), pp. 141–151; see also "The Listening Guide: A Contemporary Review of the Method and the Methodology," *Qualitative Psychology* 8/2 (2021), special issue, guest editor C. Gilligan.

13 See Gilligan et al., "Cartography of a Lost Time."

14 *The Diary of Anne Frank: The Critical Edition* (New York: Doubleday, 1989).

15 L. O. Rogers and N. Way, "Child Development in an Ideological Context: Through the Lens of Resistance and Accommodation," *Child Development Perspectives* 15/4 (December 2021), pp. 242–248.

16 M. Garcia, *We Are Not Born Submissive: How Patriarchy Shapes Women's Lives* (Princeton, NJ: Princeton University Press, 2021).

17 For the published version of this talk see J. Petrucelli,
S. Schoen, and N. Snider (eds.), *Patriarchy and its Discontents* (New York: Routledge, 2022), pp. 174–205.

18 S. B. Hrdy, *Mothers and Others: The Evolutionary
Origins of Mutual Understanding* (Cambridge, MA:
Harvard University Press, 2009). See also F. de Waal,
The Age of Empathy (New York: Harmony, 2009);
M. D. Lieberman, *Social: Our Brains are Wired to
Connect* (New York: Random House, 2013).

19 Greta Thunberg on Twitter, September 26, 2021.

20 Audre Lorde, *Your Silence Will Not Protect You*
(London: Silver Press, 2017).

21 C. Gilligan, *The Birth of Pleasure* (New York: Knopf,
2002), pp. 47–53.

**Chapter 2: Why Nobody Talks about the Abortion
Decisions**

1 V. Woolf, "Professions for Women," in *The Death
of the Moth and Other Essays* (New York: Harcourt
Brace Jovanovich, 1942[1931]), p. 237.

2 L. Kohlberg, *The Psychology of Moral Development*
(New York: Harper and Row, 1984).

3 C. Gilligan, "In a Different Voice: Women's Conceptions
of Self and of Morality," *Harvard Educational Review*
47/4 (1977), pp. 481–517: p. 491.

4 M. L. King, "Letter from Birmingham Jail," 1963;
John Donne, "No Man Is an Island," 1624.

5 C. Gilligan, *In a Different Voice: Psychological Theory
and Women's Development* (Cambridge, MA: Harvard
University Press, 1982), p. 66.

6 Ibid., p. 71.

7 Ibid., p. 100.

8 Ibid., pp. 99–100.

9 S. Laugier, "Carol Gilligan: What Gender Does to Moral Philosophy," in E. Le Jallé and A. Benoit (eds.), *Thinking with Women Philosophers: Critical Essays in Practical Contemporary Philosophy* (Geneva: Springer, 2022), pp. 8–10.

10 Ibid., p. 4.

11 Wittgenstein quoted in ibid., p. 16.

12 Ibid., p. 3.

13 Ibid., pp. 1–3.

14 Ibid., p. 2.

Chapter 3: Enter Eve

1 J. Breuer and S. Freud, "Studies on Hysteria," in *The Standard Edition*, vol. 2, 1893–95.

2 Ibid., p. 152.

3 Ibid., p. 157.

4 Ibid., pp. 110–111.

5 J. Piaget, "Introduction," *The Child's Conception of the World*, trans. Joan and Andrew Tomlinson (New York: Rowman & Littlefield, 2007[1926]).

6 A. Lorde, "The Master's Tools Will Never Dismantle the Master's House" (1979), in *Sister Outsider* (Berkeley, CA: Ten Speed Press, 1984), pp. 111–114.

7 The Holy Bible: King James Version (1611), Gen. 3:17.

8 R. Alter, *The Hebrew Bible: A Translation with Commentary* (New York: W. W. Norton, 2018), p. 16.

9 Alter, *The Hebrew Bible*, p. 17; King James Version, Gen. 3:17.

10 King James Version, p. 2 Gen. 2:18; New English Bible, p. 3; Alter, *The Hebrew Bible*, p. 14.

11 T. Morrison. *Beloved* (New York: Vintage, 2007[1987]), p. 149.

12 Ibid., p. 148.

13 Ibid., p. 86.
14 Ibid., pp. 149–150.
15 C. Alter, S. Haynes, and J. Worland., "Greta Thunberg. *Time* 2019 Person of the Year," *Time,* December 23–30, 2019, pp. 50–65: p. 58.
16 Greta Thunberg. TEDxStockholm. "The disarming case to act right now on climate change." YouTube video, 2018.
17 Alter et al., "Greta Thunberg," p. 58.
18 Ibid.
19 Ibid.
20 Ibid.
21 Ibid., p. 54.
22 W. E. B. DuBois, *The Souls of Black Folk* (New York: Oxford University Press, 2007[1903]), pp. 2–3.
23 G. R. Uter, "BoysIIMen." Paper written for the resisting injustice seminar, NYU School of Law, 2019.
24 F. de Waal, *The Age of Empathy* (New York: Harmony, 2009).
25 See J. Gilligan, *Violence: Reflections on a National Epidemic* (New York: Vintage, 1997).
26 J. Dorney, "Splitting the World Open: Connections among Women Teaching Girls," in N. Way, A. Ali, C. Gilligan, and P. Noguera (eds.), *The Crisis of Connection: Roots, Consequences, and Solutions* (New York: NYU Press, 2018), pp. 322–344.
27 Ibid., p. 342.

Chapter 4: Moral Injury

1 J. Shay, *Achilles in Vietnam: Combat Trauma and the Undoing of Character* (New York: Scribner, 1994), pp. 3–4.
2 Ibid., p. 4.

3 Ibid., pp. 4–5.
4 Ibid., p. 4.
5 L. M. Brown and C. Gilligan, *Meeting at the Crossroads: Women's Psychology and Girls' Development* (Cambridge, MA: Harvard University Press, 1992), pp. 5–6.
6 Shay, *Achilles in Vietnam*, p. 5.
7 Brown and Gilligan, *Meeting at the Crossroads*, p. 117.
8 Ibid., pp. 136–137.
9 Ibid., p. 138.
10 N. Way, *Deep Secrets: Boys' Friendships and the Crisis of Connection* (Cambridge, MA: Harvard University Press, 2011), p. 19.
11 Ibid., pp. 12, 21.
12 Ibid., p. 242.
13 Ibid., p. 1.
14 C. Brontë, *Jane Eyre* (New York: Penguin, 2006[1847]), pp. 44–45.
15 Ibid., p. 45.
16 For an analysis of the differences between the three versions of Anne Frank's diary (her actual diary, her edited version, and the first published version edited by her father), and also the cut made at the request of her father, see C. Gilligan, "Regions of Light," in *The Birth of Pleasure* (New York: Knopf, 2002), pp. 85–113.
17 J. B. Miller and I. Stiver. *The Healing Connection: How Women Form Relationships in Therapy and in Life* (Boston, MA: Beacon Press, 1997).
18 Judy Y. Chu, *When Boys Become Boys: Development, Relationships, and Masculinity* (New York: NYU Press, 2014), p. 209.
19 Ibid., p. 108.

20 D. Moss, *Thirteen Ways of Looking at a Man* (New York: Routledge, 2012), pp. 137–141.

21 Ibid., p. 141.

22 L. Tolstoy, *Anna Karenina*, trans. R. Pevear and L. Volokhonsky (New York: Viking, 2001[1877]).

23 A. Roy, *The God of Small Things* (New York: Random House, 2017[1997]), p. 168.

24 N. Hawthorne, *The Scarlet Letter* (New York: Penguin, 1986[1850]), pp. 18, 20, 190.

25 Tolstoy, *Anna Karenina*, p. 410.

26 Ibid., p. 435.

27 Ibid., pp. 418–419.

28 Ibid., p. 414.

29 I am indebted to Carole Obedin for pointing this out.

30 Tolstoy, *Anna Karenina*, p. 419.

31 Ibid.

32 Ibid., p. 425.

33 Ibid., p. 429.

Chapter 5: In a Different Voice: Act II

1 *Fresh Air*. Paul Thomas Anderson and Terry Gross on *Phantom Thread*, January 23, 2018.

2 P. Schrader, "In Writing 'First Reformed,' an Intellectual Decision Soon Became Overwhelmingly Emotional," *Los Angeles Times*, January 2, 2019; see also A. Wilkinson, "Paul Schrader on *First Reformed*: "This Is a Troubling Film about a Troubled Person," *Vox*, June 18, 2018; and E. Cortellessa, "Paul Schrader on *First Reformed*'s Provocative Ending and Its Many Influences," *Slate*, June 13, 2018.

3 A. O. Scott, "Spike Lee's 'BlacKkKlansman' Journeys into White AMERICA's Heart of Darkness," *The New York Times*, August 9, 2018; Rembert Browne, "Spike

Lee wants BlacKkKlansman to Wake America Up," *Time,* August 9, 2018.

Epilogue: The Ethic of Care

1 J. Berger, *G.: A Novel* (New York: Vintage, 1972); C. Gilligan, *In a Different Voice: Psychological Theory and Women's Development* (Cambridge, MA: Harvard University Press, 1982); A. Roy, *The God of Small Things* (New York: Random House, 2017[1997]).
2 L. M. Brown and C. Gilligan, *Meeting at the Crossroads: Women's Psychology and Girls' Development* (Cambridge, MA: Harvard University Press, 1992), pp. 31–32.

Index

Index

children
  development of 41
  gender codes 12, 15, 16
  healthy resistance 29–30,
    108
  initiation, process of
    11–12, 14, 15, 16, 66–7
  masculinity and femininity
    11–12, 30–1
  morality and 11
  relationships 12–13, 31
  voices of 43, 83–4
  well-being 18
children's voices 43, 83–4
*The Child's Conception of
  the World* (Piaget) 57
Chu, Judy 30–1, 76, 77–9,
  86–7
climate change 48, 67, 68–9
clinical interrogatory
  (*méthode clinique*) 57
Clinton, Hillary 24–5
Close (dir. Lukas Dhont)
  109
cognitive development 13,
  47
Colorado College 103
Colvin, Claudette 30, 117n9
combat veterans 73–4, 77
connection 72
  crisis of 12–13, 15
consciousness 86
contradictions 36
cover voice 23, 29, 30, 33,
  35, 44, 45, 110
crisis of connection 12–13,
  15
  see also Deep Secrets:

*Boys' Friendships and
  the Crisis of Connection*
  (Way)
cultural relativism 3
curiosity 32, 110

Damasio, Antonio 13
Dangaremba, Tsi Tsi 83
Day-Lewis, Daniel 94, 95
*Deep Secrets: Boys'
  Friendships and the
  Crisis of Connection*
  (Way) 12, 76, 79–81,
  109
democracy
  equal voice 19
  patriarchy and 19, 82
depression 14
  flip-flop 14
Dhont, Lukas 109
Didion, Joan 49
different voice 2, 7, 8–9,
  53–4, 105, 106, 107,
  110
  Eve (biblical) 66
In a Different Voice
  (Gilligan) 1–2, 6–7, 8,
  17, 19, 28, 48, 105,
  106–7, 110
disruption 7–8
dissociation 17, 29, 31, 32,
  58, 66–7, 86
dissociative 21
distinctive voice 106–7
Dobbs *v.* Jackson Women's
  Health Organization
  (2022) 2, 19
Donne, John 48

Index

Index

Index

Parks, Rosa 30, 117n9
Patmore, Coventry 47
patriarchy 12, 13, 15, 104,
    107, 110
  blind complicity 39
  definition 15
  democracy and 19, 82
  double consciousness 70–1
  gender binary and
      hierarchy 9, 10, 11, 14,
      15–16, 29–30, 82, 107
  ideologies of 44
  male superiority 39
  resistance to 20–1, 25,
      29–30, 65
  shaky psychological
      foundation 18
  social constructionism 70
  struggle of men 70
  unnaturalness of 82
  violence and silence 18
Phantom Thread (dir. Paul
    Thomas Anderson) 94,
    95–9
Piaget, Jean 5, 9, 47, 57
political resistance 30
psyche 82–3, 107
psychoanalysis 57, 58
psychological inquiry 57
psychological resistance 30
psychology 3, 58
  women and 5, 7–8

racial agnosia 38–9
racism 38
radical listening 31, 32–4
  definition 32
  under voice 35, 44

Radio Free Orange 85
Real, Terrence 43
real thoughts 22, 23, 33,
    34–5, 44, 45, 81
relational betrayal 42
relational knowing 39–40
relationships
  betrayal 76
  children and 12–13
  inner silence 81
  insoluble problems of 36
  sacrificing 86, 107
  self and 13, 16, 29
resilience 13, 14
resistance 30, 69, 108
  accommodation and 31,
      36–7
  of children 29–30, 108
  of girls 14–15, 109
  healthy 30
  to moral injury 106
  to patriarchy 20–1, 25,
      29–30, 65
  political 30
  psychological 30
responsible behavior 50, 51,
    53
Richards, David 10
right *see* "what's right"
Roe *v.* Wade (1973) 2–3, 4,
    19, 28, 46, 49
Rogers, Leoandra Onnie 36,
    37
A Room of One's Own
    (Woolf) 7
Roy, Arundhati 17, 83, 88,
    106
Rudolph, Maya 95

Index